Teaching Matters

General Editors: Sydney Hill and Colin Reid

Teaching Poetry in the Secondary School

Veronica O'Brien
University College, Dublin

Edward Arnold

© Veronica O'Brien 1985

First published in Great Britain 1985
by Edward Arnold (Publishers) Ltd,
41 Bedford Square, London WC1B 3DQ

Edward Arnold (Australia) Pty Ltd,
80 Waverley Road, Caulfield East,
Victoria 3145, Australia.

British Cataloguing in Publication Data

O'Brien Veronica
    Teaching poetry in the secondary school.—
    (Teaching matters)
    1. English literature—Study and teaching
    (Secondary)
    I. Title   II. Series
    821'.007'12   PR33

ISBN 0–7131–8271–7

Text set in 10/11 Baskerville
by The Word Factory Limited, Rossendale, Lancashire.
Printed and Bound in Great Britain by
Whitstable Litho Ltd., Whitstable, Kent

General Editors' Preface

The books in this series provide information and advice on a wide range of educational issues for teachers who are busy, yet who are concerned to keep abreast of new developments.

The aim is practicality: slim volumes that are sources of authoritative help and swift reference, written and edited by people whose expertise in their field is backed up by experience of the everyday realities of school and classroom. The books are planned to cover well-defined topics relevant to schools in widely differing situations: subject teaching, curriculum development, areas of responsibility within schools, and the relationship of the school to the community. They are published at a time when there is a growing call for increased professional accountability in our primary and secondary schools. The 'in-service between covers' that characterizes these handbooks is designed to contribute to the vitality and development of schools and of the individuals within them.

Asked if our preference was for teaching the novel, drama or poetry, the vast majority of English teachers would opt for one of the first two. Relatively few would favour poetry. The reasons for this are many, but significant among them must be the special 'challenge' of much 'good' poetry, the resistance of many pupils to it, the gaps in our own knowledge, lack of familiarity with a large enough selection of material that *works* in the classroom and having little confidence that we possess the strategies and techniques necessary to make it enjoyable and absorbing.

In this book, Veronica O'Brien provides clear solutions to these and many other problems associated with teaching poetry and does so with an infectious enthusiasm for her subject and a practicality that will encourage the wary and suggest new approaches to the experienced.

Acknowledgements

The author and publishers would like to thank the following for permission to include copyright material:

Faber and Faber Publishers for 'Fan-Piece, for Her Imperial Lord' from Ezra Pound: *Collected Shorter Poems* and 'The Snow Man' from Wallace Stevens: *The Collected Poems of Wallace Stevens*, and Jonathan Cape Ltd and Holt, Rinehart and Winston, Publishers for 'The Pasture' from *The Poetry of Robert Frost* edited by Edward Connery Lathem. Copyright 1939 © 1967, 1969 by Holt, Rinehart and Winston and reprinted by permission.

Contents

Formal comment: teaching the elements
Draft work: second stage
Thinking points and the individual draft record
Handling an 'unseen' poem
Writing up a draft record

Sampling a poetry course
Poetry seminars
Voice and vision
Unwriting a poem
A reader and a poet

1

'Every child may joy to hear'

(William Blake)

This book is based on the belief that Blake is right. The capacity to be moved by a work of art is a natural human gift. Blake's children were the children of the London poor, abused, neglected, 'reduc'd to misery' (*London*), not a privileged few. The possible 'joy' ranges widely—from being prompted to laughter or pity or anger to being brought to silence; from recognition of a brightened scrap of the familiar world to the sense of being a 'dweller in possibility'; from the satisfaction of 'That's it, that's what I feel' to the surprise of 'I never thought of that before'; from the pleasure of quickened senses to the pleasure of a leap of the mind, and so on. There is wide variation in what moves different people and in the ability to articulate what is felt and known. But the capacity itself is a common possession. The right to participate in the achievements of the imaginative arts, in what Stuart Hampshire calls 'glory' (**1**), is everyone's right. So we bring art into the classroom.

Unlike other kinds of knowledge we bring in, the knowledge available in art cannot be adapted, broken down and handed out in units of progressive difficulty. Like the boy's head in Miroslav Holub's poem —and like the heads of the children in the desks—'it just cannot be trimmed' (*A Boy's Head*). There is great comfort in this for the teacher. Participation does not depend on having a good brain or a good memory or a facility for absorbing information. It does not mean being able to give measurable evidence of participation. The act is essentially unmeasurable, 'felt in the blood and felt along the heart'. In this area it is not our job to bring pupils to some measurable standard of performance, but to make a clear space for the 'joy' to happen, for intuition, imagination, feeling—those secret common powers—to play with the poem or the picture or the music.

Time affects the way we are moved. In childhood, participation is participation in an exercise which is not questioned. Young children chant the rhyme, dance to the music, laugh at the colours. Later, as reflective powers develop, participation is more complex, and so more difficult to handle in the classroom—the only place where many meet art. The chanting, the dancing, the laughing are still the essential core, even though they may now be wholly internal. Art is not art for the child (**2**); it begins to become art in adolescence when the experience stirs not only participation but reflection. The difficulty is in freeing a reflection which is itself a kind of joy.

A shared language

The art-form we are concerned with is poetry, the form whose medium is language. Reader and poet can therefore meet from the very beginning on common ground—the ground of a shared language. The language of poetry is not a category, a special professional register. 'Its only essential difference from conversation is that it is much more memorable' (**3**). A poet draws on all the resources of a language; he does not invent a new one, but brings to light possibilities within the shared system. The organization is organization of patterns already there. Before the difference between the language of a poem and what we think of as ordinary language, there is the similarity. Rhyme, rhythm, metaphor, short cuts, twists of syntax, and so on are natural tendencies of language revealed in ordinary everyday use as well as in formal poetic use.

Observation of young children while they are acquiring language is one way of seeing how naturally poets and non-poets meet. The freshness of the small child's experiments reminds us that there is a period when all users resemble poets in energy of effort and in readiness to test out the possibilities. What the child comes up with is the result of incomplete knowledge; what the poet arrives at is the result of deliberate attentiveness. But both ventures throw light on the workings of language and alert us to its inexhaustibility. The language we think we have caught up on is still ahead, still being made; not merely in the obvious sense of new names for new things, but in the sense of new attempts to articulate common human experience, the felt knowledge of being alive.

The poet reminds us of the creativity of language (**4**). In poetry 'words have no banisters' (**5**). Meaning does not stop at the edge of the dictionary definition. This is why 'poetry can communicate before it is understood' (**6**), and can communicate with a variety of readers. Again, young children show an intuitive grasp of the openness of meaning in poetic language. Few nursery rhymes offer a hold on the verifiable world. Babylon and candlelight name nothing actual in the child's experience. Something beyond the actual is being learned—that langauge is not limited to making statements about the obvious.

Poetry and the growth of language power

The possession of language enables the user to build 'a duplicate world' within the mind (**7**). Ability to do so adequately depends on the range of language of which the user has experience. In adolescence, as the growth of various powers accelerates, there is need for language experience which keeps pace with the growth. The development of reasoning power demands an increased emphasis on training in the language of rational discourse, what might be called paraphraseable language.

There is an equal need for language which keeps pace with and encourages the growth of powers equally important in the advance towards personal freedom and personal responsibility: the powers of the unparaphraseable self – intuition, feeling, imagination. Poetry answers this need, for it is there that we find 'language at full stretch' (**8**), able to build a duplicate world which is 'incorrigibly plural'(**9**).

We cannot measure the effect of poetry on the growth of language power as we can measure the effect of lessons on the rules of grammar or clear statement. The fact that we cannot measure the effect does not mean that there is none. There is, I believe, a long-term effect on the ability to go 'beyond the information given'. Because the words of poetry 'have no banisters', a network of hidden relationships is brought into sight, the experience of which sharpens the reader's own skill to perceive relationships.

> I'm going out to clean the pasture spring;
> I'll only stop to rake the leaves away
> (And wait to watch the water clear, I may):
> I shan't be gone long. You come too.
>
> I'm going out to fetch the little calf
> That's standing by the mother. It's so young
> It totters when she licks it with her tongue.
> I shan't be gone long. You come too.

The Pasture (Robert Frost)

'Poetry' says Frost, 'begins in delight and makes a little run to a bit of wisdom' (**10**). The mind that takes in that poem takes in much more than information about a farmer's work. The relations enacted in the poem—dullness and clearness, vulnerability and stability, non-human instinct and human awareness and tenderness—are taken in because the effect of the language is to 'make the water clear' so that the reader too 'makes a little run to wisdom'. The young reader may not be able to explain what he feels intuitively. His understanding is performed in the pleasure and ease of participation. For a moment he becomes the poet. It may be only for a moment, but language life is nourished by such moments.

A distinctive characteristic of poetry is its accessibility to all sorts of learners. On a practical level, there is the huge number of poems small enough in size to get easily through the classroom door. This offers a range of choice not possible with the other language arts where the amount of time available limits the amount of variety we can provide. One of the most difficult tasks in writing this book was selecting poems for illustration, as there was so much to choose from. I have confined myself to poems which appear in most school anthologies and which I have found to work in different kinds of classroom. (A selection of the anthologies used is given in the index of poems.) Even within those restrictions there were always several others asking to be chosen from which another teacher would have made a different selection.

The main reason for the accessibility of poetry is its power to 'communicate before it is understood'. This means that the young reader, whatever his measurable intelligence, can find and enjoy his own level of communication with a poem. We have to grow up before we can read *Middlemarch*, but not before we can hear *The Tyger*. There are of course poems we have to grow up to, but the number is small enough in relation to the number we can start growing with in childhood and adolescence.

There is another characteristic of poetry invaluable in education. Poetry offers young readers an open line to the past. Of all the language arts it is the one least bound by the effects of distance in time, most able to 'adapt itself to other epochs and other readerships'(11).

The experience of poetry increases the reader's awareness of his own relationship with language. It may inspire him to try for a time to write poetry himself. Finding words for what we 'see feelingly' is the most difficult of language acts, and the attempt to do so is of great value in the growth of personal language power. But whether the attempt is made or not, there is great value in being able to hear language that 'sees feelingly'. The act quickens as well as satisfies our own seeing power and helps to keep alive the capacity to be delighted by surprise. 'The inability to be delighted by surprise [in language] is both a misfortune for the whole of the society in which it occurs and a personal disaster for the individual who suffers it'(12).

The teacher's role

A student teacher remembered her dismay at the first poetry lesson when she went up to secondary school. The teacher put a list of technical terms on the blackboard, asked the pupils to explain them, and when they failed to do so told them they had a lot to learn. Such an approach turns the job upside down, tries to sell bits of an engine in place of an engine which works.

The teacher rather than print is the mediator between a poem and a group of listeners, the presenter of an object that 'begins in delight'. We cannot teach delight. What we try to do is to create conditions in which delight can happen.

The primary appeal is to the intuitive powers, to imagination and feeling. The intuitive nature of what is being presented requires us to bring our own intuitive powers into play. The poem is not treated as a peculiar form of comprehension exercise with a neatly defined goal of improving reading and writing skills. We need to clear our minds of preconceptions based on the pupils' performance in other kinds of learning. What is most valuable perhaps is belief in the particularity of the people in the desks, in their irreducible eachness.

The less pedagogic anxiety brought to the task, the more the poem is trusted to do its own teaching, the greater the chance of success. What is most deeply learned is after all beyond our reach. What pupils in time learn to articulate about the experience at any level is only the tip of the iceberg. Eventually many will need to show evidence of their knowledge in an examination of some kind. They are better disposed to learn to do so if they enjoy taking in the poetry itself.

Naturalness is a vital quality, an attitude that takes it for granted that there is nothing odd about writing or reading a poem. Poetry should enter the classroom 'as naturally as the leaves come to a tree'(**13**). Piosity—anything that smacks of This-is-Beautiful-Thoughts-in-Beautiful-Language—hardens suspicion in the doubtful and encourages gush in the docile. Another unprofitable practice is treating a poem as a piece of work which has to be graded good, not so good, bad. 'True personal discrimination or taste develops slowly and probably best unconsciously. It cannot be forced by exercises in selecting the good and rejecting the bad: it may indeed be stunted. It comes, if it is to come at all, by growth in understanding and enjoyment of the good'(**14**).

Naturalness is extremely important in the way a poem is read aloud. Most children cannot take a new poem cold from the page; some are alarmed simply by the fact that it is in print. Reading aloud rescues the poem from the trap of print, retrieves it for the ear. The teacher's live reading is preferable to a recording and it is worth developing the skill of reading well, which does not mean developing a special poetry voice. Recordings have their uses (see chapter 3) but they should be used sparingly. The machine with its 'foreign' accent can be a source of distraction rather than a means of focusing attention on the poem itself.

The teacher's own attitude to poetry is always active. Our interest, our pleasure, our grown capacity to be moved are a powerful influence, however open we rightly try to be. Openness is a matter of being ready to attend freshly to the familiar and fairly to the unfamiliar, of being ready to exploit the variety of choice. We should beware, I think, of too much playing safe. Our pupils do not have to like everything we like. The hope is to provide a range wide enough for all to discover what pleases them. It is wise never to underestimate the poetic reach of any class. Young people frequently upset our notions of what is appropriate for their age and taste. The more variety we can offer, the better. In any classroom there is a great diversity of people. It may be that many people never come to think of poetry as a source of pleasure because they did not meet in their school life the poem which for them would have been a flash of the sudden sun.

2

'I, too, dislike it'

(Marianne Moore)

Hostility to poetry is so common a phenomenon in the secondary school that it cannot be put down to lack of ability or to earlier disagreeable experience of the art. Children of all kinds who a short time before responded with ease and interest pull back uneasily. It is not simply a matter of suspicion of what teachers value. Drama and story do not cause the same degree of discomfort, frequently masked as contempt. There are, I think, two main reasons. One reason is that the challenge of the unknown, the unfamiliar, is more obvious in poetry than in the other forms of literature encountered. The move from the certainties of childhood to the uncertainties of adolescence brings with it a great urge to be able to know, able to master the parts. As the ability to analyze increases, so does the recognition of difficulties in the way poetic language behaves, which earlier did not bother pupils at all. Poems become a potential threat to self-esteem. The other reason is the challenge of what is just beginning to be known, to be familiar: the resurgence of feeling more intense than it has been since infancy(**15**), and the uncomfortable business of developing self-awareness. Drama and story set these challenges too, but they appear to be more manageable, more reducible to other terms, to provide more wearable masks. There are obvious footholds; something definable can be done with them. A play can be acted; a story can be read; a plot can be abstracted; characters can be judged. Again, because the mode is people in interaction, drama and story do not, on the surface, appear to demand separation from the safety of the group.

The way we approach poetry seeks to remove the false barrier of alarm. It is not so much a matter of restoring confidence as of fostering a new confidence in new strengths, new powers of thinking and feeling, which the experience of poetry both challenges and satisfies.

'Tell all the truth but tell it slant'

In this situation we need to be especially vigilant that no sacred cows are lumbering after us into the classroom, festooned with enthusiastic recommendations. To attempt to explain the value and pleasure of poetry merely hardens suspicion. The young dislike sermons. Interest in poetry grows through experience of the thing itself. Our contribution is not to plead the cause of poetry, but to create a context in which it has a chance to speak for itself.

'Success in circuit lies'. Slant tactics are called for, a way of smuggling in poetry so that the experience can occur while the main object of attention is something else. When trying to naturalize poetry in the classroom, I should avoid altogether formal poetry lessons or frontal attacks on a set book, and try to arrange matters so that poems are present for their contribution to activity that is interesting for other reasons. In the approach I have in mind, poems are never studied in the conventional sense; there is no explicit attention to poems as poems. The focus of attention is not the activity of the poem, but the activity of the pupils which the poem serves. At the same time, since the various strategies used have their roots in the craft of poetry, a foundation is being laid for a different kind of attention later, when doubts have been allayed.

The strategies that follow are outlined separately for convenience of description. In practice there is a great deal of cross-over. There is no special virtue in the order in which strategies are described. Where to start is a matter for the individual teacher to decide, with his unique knowledge of the chemistry of the group of pupils. Poems are suggested in connection with the different strategies (see appendix); readers will make their own substitutions, in the light of their own taste as well as their knowledge of their pupils. The number of poems introduced at a given moment varies according to the demands of a strategy and the interest of the class.

Patience is perhaps what one needs most in trying to naturalize poetry where it is seen as alien. It is important not to force the pace. Progress is seldom neat; one can seldom predict the high points and the low points. The low points may not be as low as they seem; signs that a poem has struck home may surface long after its introduction; poems rejected during one activity may be accepted during another. Pupils must feel free to take or leave a poem. At all points, they are involved in choice; there needs to be enough material available to make the choice real. A single school anthology is unsatisfactory for this purpose; a practical solution is to draw on a number of anthologies.

Noises on and off

Linking music and poetry is a simpler matter in the junior school than in the secondary school. It is possible to catch the attention of ten-year-olds with music outside their experience and make this the source of a variety of experiments with the rhythmic life of language. The possibilities are much more limited with older children and it takes a strong head to use the approach. The trouble is that one is confined to whatever music is currently approved by the pupils, which may or may not be profitable material for experiment. At the same time, the popularity of using music makes it worth trying as an approach, as a lead-in to other forms of work with sound.

Words for music

The Elizabethan practice of fitting words to music rather than the other way round can be adapted to the classroom. The material to use is non-vocal music—the B side of a single, or non-vocal instrumental pieces. The choice can be made by the pupils. How a title—often divergent and riddling—matches a piece is a starting-point for discussion. Suggestions for alternative titles are canvassed on the basis of the associations a piece evokes for different listeners—images, feelings, situations. These suggestions become the raw material for creating an accompanying lyric. A key word or phrase is chosen which will recur frequently in the manner of popular music; the key word determines other selections from the raw material. Combinations of the selected language are tried out against the music until there is general satisfaction with the arrangement. The result is recorded.

A variation is to beat out the rhythm of a selected piece vocally, using meaningless syllables, and then to translate these into words, any words at all, which then become the key words for a lyric. Another variation is to take a casual remark, a pause-filler, a current catch phrase, and see what can be made out of it to match a piece of music. For example, the phrase 'anything you say' can be expanded into a lyric.

The next experiment is to match a given pattern of words to a piece of non-vocal music. It might be worth starting with that form of Dub Reggae where the singer chants poetry over the instrumental backing track of another song. This would serve as an introduction to using pieces of verse as words for music. The pieces can be very short; they should contain repetition or suggest it, and be elastic enough to be pulled into different rhythmic shape. To start with, it is best to choose pieces unfamiliar to the pupils. The pupils select the music to match the verse. A performance of the words as an accompaniment to the music is worked out; this is a matter of highlighting keywords or echowords, pacing repetitions or supplying new ones, varying pitch. Spoken rather than chanted performance is effective, and alerts performers to the possibilities of the speaking voice.

A further development—and a way out to other work—is to set small groups working on their own selection from a number of pieces provided by the teacher. This makes it possible to introduce varied material which allows for different levels of sophistication.

Sound poems

A sound poem is a construction which explores the phonic content of a word or phrase and its emotive associations, or which uses language and sound effects to create a small drama on a given theme or incident. The work is fascinating and leads to discovery of the music buried in everyday speech and to a satisfying discipline of activity.

To start, a recording of a sound poem is played to the class. This could be a piece created by another class, or, if one is starting from scratch, a piece created with the aid of interested senior pupils or colleagues. For example, the starting word *Shout* might yield the following shape:

> 1)   The word as a whole repeated in various ways—in unison, in disunion, at full pitch, in a whisper.
> 2)   The word broken in two: *sh* prolonged, followed by *out* staccato; the pattern repeated a few times.
> 3)   The word beheaded: *ou* prolonged, followed abruptly by *t*.
> 4)   The hiss of the opening *sh* and the meaning of *out* might inspire creating a small drama of someone being excluded from the group.

No special equipment is needed, apart from a way of recording results. The emphasis is on discovering the context of sound and situation a word or phrase can generate. Transformations, echoes, contrasts are chosen for their appropriateness to the drama emerging. Thus, *rout* or *clout* might appear in developing the above example.

In the experiment above, a theme is found in the phonic exploration. Another way of creating a sound poem is to start with a theme and find words and sounds to give the theme concrete shape. Themes are taken from the everyday world—*In the Kitchen, At the Bus-stop, Clocks, Sleep, Homework*. Once they have become interested in the work, pupils are ingenious at suggesting themes. The experiment starts with collecting various associations called up by the theme and then selecting the most promising and practicable. This material is ordered into a set of sequences. For example, the theme *Sleep* took the form:

> 1)   Trying to get to sleep.
> 2)   Falling asleep.
> 3)   Dreaming.
> 4)   Snoring.
> 5)   Coming out of sleep.

The challenge is to select words and sounds to convey the sensation of an experience. In the *Sleep* piece, the falling asleep sequence started with a babble produced by playing a tape at the wrong speed. This was followed by repeating the word 'hush' to suggest the regular swish of waves, and this gave way to a high humming note to suggest entry into the other world of dreaming. Emphasis is on finding a coherent shape, using recurrent key words and sounds to give unity to the whole. Words are limited in number, and chosen for sound as much as sense. The

pupils' ingenuity is challenged into action. In the *Sleep* piece, the
snoring was created by two pupils; one providing the snort, the other
the whistle.

The technique is then turned to transcribing a poem into a sound
poem. The teacher provides a set of poems; the pupils choose which to
work on. Poems are mined for ideas for activity. The work leads to
active participation in the craft of a poem, picking up the pattern of
sound, playing with echoes, attending to arrangement. Pupils are encouraged to do things to the poem; the aim is that they should create
something themselves. A general guiding rule is that the transcription
should pick up the words, shape, mood of the original. But the rule is
flexible. The resulting version may use the whole poem with accompanying sounds, or may use only selected key words to point the new
sounds. Details in the poem may be replaced by details selected by the
creators as truer to their own experience of life.

Connections

The purpose is to set working visual imagination, to increase agility in
seeing from the word. Before attending to the poet's connections, pupils
are set to discovering the connections going on under the surface of
their own minds and bringing them to the forefront of consciousness.
The constant underlying aim is to cause awareness of the amount and
variety of connective imagining any mind engages in minute by minute.

The starting-point is direct observation of some object. For example,
in one experiment the classroom was darkened. A piece of Venetian
glass was placed in front of the blackboard and a torch was played on it
so that moving reflections appeared on the board. The game is to
discover the connections made by different observers. To start with, all
that is asked for is first thoughts, and the connections may be vague
and formless. Then the challenge is made more precise—to find the
image, the sense-object, the picture in the mind. 'It's like . . .', 'I'd
connect it with . . .', 'It makes me think of . . .'. The teacher is one of
the players. Contributions are collected and recorded on the board.
Then a few of these are selected to start off another set of connections;
or each player chooses someone else's connection and makes another.
Now connections are being made from words not objects.

When a number of experiments has been tried, energy is turned from
subjective exploration to objective creation. The set of assorted connections produced by one experiment is used as material for creating a
language object. A central item is decided on and other items are
selected or rejected on the basis of their fitting in with this centre. The
exercise frequently generates new perceptions. Shape is evolved
through deliberate repetition of the central item or variations on it.
Another possibility is the game of chain-reaction. This is an exercise

which matches occasions where the initial connections tend to be similar. One experiment which began with water in a pottery bowl with a design on the base finished in a chain-reaction piece entitled 'How did we get to dolphins?'

The next stage is to use poetry as a source of connections, choosing short poems or extracts with a strong visual content. With some classes, Wallace Stevens's *Thirteen Ways of Looking at a Blackbird* can be used as a bridge to this stage. If the Stevens poem is judged too difficult for the class, Peter Redgrove's imitation *Thirteen Ways of Looking at a Blackboard* is a simple alternative. The pupils put together sets of thirteen connections chosen from experiments already worked, making sure that every member of the class is represented in the final collection.

When a poem is used, it is important to keep the emphasis on the pupils' activity. The connections which they make are the centre of attention, not those the poem makes. Connections are invited for the poem or extract as a whole, or the class selects one image to be the starting object. In each case what follows is producing a set of connections as in previous experiments, and creating from these a new 'poem'. The activity can be further developed in individual work, each choosing a detail from a poem and exploring the connections it starts up. The exercise causes much livelier attention to a poem than the 'say-what-line-you-like-best' type.

Seeing a poem

Conscious exploration of the way imagination naturally goes into action in response to sense perception opens the way for closer sharing in the seeing that poetic language makes possible. The focus is shifted from finding new personal connections to trying to see through the poet's eyes. Two kinds of poetic seeing are used: poems in which an object is isolated, which use detail sparingly; poems in which background as well as foreground is filled in, where detail is dense. The pupils do not look at the text, but depend on hearing only.

An example of the first kind is *The Red Wheelbarrow* (William Carlos Williams). The only details are the wheelbarrow, the white chickens, the glaze of rain-water. The reading should obey the pacing the line-arrangement indicates. What the pupils try to do is simply to watch what happens as they take in the picture. The emphasis is on the amount the individual hearer contributes to the scene, the connections he makes from the poet's words.

The other kind of seeing suggests a different emphasis—on getting into focus the multiple details given. This time the aim is to re-compose the picture the *poet* sees, watching what *he* watches, following the direction of *his* eyes. For example, John Clare's *The Badger*. Whether the whole poem is read first depends on the attention-stamina of the class.

It might be wise to choose one paragraph only to start with. The class chooses one line as the centre of the picture; the background is filled in from the other lines. For example, the third paragraph which describes the baiting of the captured badger. The likely centre picture is 'The badger grins and never leaves his hold'. Around this image the rest is filled in, using the idea of a framed painting with its different areas: right-hand, left-hand, upper, lower, foreground, background, near, distant . . . Only Clare's details are used: houses, dogs, mastiff licking his feet, bulldog, crowd; the activity of the crowd—stone-throwing, urging the dogs on, flying from the badger, the reeling drunkard. Each detail is given a precise place as the picture is re-composed verbally. If the teacher judges interest to be sufficient, other details may be added by drawing on other parts of the poem: the poacher, the scampering dogs, the frightened woman, the woods. Or another picture is re-composed from another paragraph.

Clare's poetry provides excellent material for this kind of work because of the intentness of observation and his genius for showing plain. Every line says, Look here, and here, and here. His work has the immediate clarity of a TV nature film and pupils can learn to watch it with the same fascination. But there are situations where the natural world awakens no interest, or itself provokes active hostility. In such a situation, poems are better chosen whose picture is nearer home. Poems about people are one source to draw on: the analogy of the photograph is more likely to work than that of the painting.

In these exercises the picture is static. A further development is watching a moving picture. For this purpose, poems which relate an incident are chosen; there are several in most modern school anthologies. In this, the seeing emphasis is on the changing sequence, image giving place to image as in a film. Before hearing the piece, the class is told to concentrate on the way the picture moves forward. When they have heard the poem twice, they try tracing the sequence.

The work is oral: the interaction of different ways of seeing is a necessary prop and stimulus. A simple reinforcement exercise is *Cataloguing*. The class is given a set of poems and extracts without titles. Working in small groups, they divide these into three catalogues—one for paintings, one for photographs, one for films. The decision on how to catalogue a piece is taken by the pupils. Entries are brief, merely indicative of type. A title is added in each case.

Sample entries
For *Winter* (Shakespeare)
'*When icicles hang by the wall*' Painting. Medium. Heavy frame. Kitchen scene in winter. Four figures: two male, two female. Open door shows snow. Large owl in top left hand corner. Title: *Cold*.
For the first stanza of *The Beach* (Robert Graves)

'Louder than gulls' Photograph. Large. Unframed. Black-and-white. Sea-side scene with children. Title: *A Day at the sea*.
For *The Clock-Winder* (Hardy)
'It is as dark as a cave' Film. Black-and-white. Mystery. Lighting dim throughout. Weird atmosphere. Title: *The Rheumatic Clock*.

A shape for feeling

Any contact with poetry is contact with emotion, brought into the open air, given a shape, expressed and examined. The experiments so far suggested involve experience of the relationship between poetry and emotion, but the relationship is not a matter for explicit attention. The emphasis is on experience, on activity; the poetry is left to work its effect in secret satisfactions. It would be unwise, given the situation we are trying to remedy, to draw the pupils' attention to the fact that they themselves are behaving poetically.

An attempt to go further in this aspect of poetry is again made with a crabwise movement. We try to make it possible for the pupils to discover the power of the poem to match personal confusions and doubts about feeling with satisfying clarity and certainty. Self-consciousness will block the path. For this reason, it is best to work with those emotions young people are not shy of talking about, such as anger, resentment, frustration. Possibilities suggest themselves in the course of other experiments. For instance, a sound poem on fighting of some kind is likely to reveal a shortage of words for conveying anger or humiliation.

Stuck for words

The experience of being stuck for words is sharply familiar to adolescents. Acceleration in the emotional life occurs without the freedom to shout and scream and kick as small children do. Early furies can be drawn on to start with ; pupils are naturally more ready to examine the emotional expression of an age-group other than their own. An account of infant anger, for example, Joyce Cary's *New Boots* (**16**), can be used to set going an experiment in observing and reporting the way small children deal with emotion. The aim is simply to give the question of strong emotion breathing-space in the classroom. All that is looked for is identification of the sort of emotional activity expressed through physical activity.

The next step is to bring the exercise nearer home. In most situations it is possible to bring the class to examine their own resources for expressing anger or frustration verbally. There is a risk in this invitation, but provided that the tone is strictly investigative and good-humoured, the risk is worth taking for the ease of relationship it establishes. Besides, the open air has a healthy, defusing effect. One does need to take account, of course, of the mixed ability of a particular class in the matter of bad language. The point of the exercise is to bring into view the monotony of available resources and the shortness of any available string of curses. The exercise can be by-passed by going straight to the way poets deal with expression of fury. A few examples of cursing poems are read to the class. Gaelic poetry provides plenty of material. The examples are used as a model for the pupils' own activity. They set about creating a string of maledictions for situations in which they are regularly stuck for words. Detention at a particularly inopportune moment, rejection of a piece of work, having a prized possession confiscated, having to stop doing something they are enjoying, specific prohibitions of authority. The construction of a string is not random: there is deliberate choice of order, of line-length, phrase-shape, rhythm, as in the models. It is an exhilarating communal exercise, and the group can usually be relied on to censor unsavoury items; feeling is attached to objects and there is a rudimentary attempt at shape.

An image for feeling

Then a more subtle kind of enactment is introduced, as feeling is transformed into a language-object which both fixes and reflects on the experience. There are two ways of approaching this. One is to start with a poem which is a dramatic image for a specific emotion—Blake's *A Poison Tree* is an obvious example—and to use the poem as a model for creating a new piece to fix a different emotion. The other way is to start with a given emotion and to find an image to match it. This approach resembles the 'connections' experiment, but differs in moving towards, not from, an object and in being more rigorously directed. Suggestions are collected—object, image or situation—to represent the given emotion. One of these is chosen for moulding into a shape which gives the emotion 'a local habitation'. The aim is to create a miniature drama. There is stress on cutting away unnecessary detail in order to sharpen the central image. The work is communal, but if interest is high it can be extended into individual work or work in small groups. The extension gives scope for the entrance of other emotions pupils are ordinarily shy of acknowledging in public.

The final stage is making a short anthology of pieces each of which is an image for an identifiable emotion. This involves pupils in a precise critical activity. In the anthology their own creations take their place with those from poems chosen by the teacher.

The experiment gives pupils the protection of a mask in confronting personal emotion, and makes it possible to introduce a range of poems one might hesitate to present 'straight'. Since identification of emotion is the only explicit challenge, they read the poems offered without alarm.

Tales of every day and every night

In the matter of naturalizing poetry, we seldom exploit sufficiently the unfailing attraction of a story at any age. We tend to think in terms of narrative verse in distinction from other kinds of verse, and overlook the story element in a large number of poems not conventionally included in the category 'narrative'. It is possible to plan a whole poetry course around the notion that every poem offered is a story — from the ballad *Sir Patrick Spens* to the three lines of *Fan-piece, for Her Imperial Lord* (Ezra Pound). A course like this has the aim of leading pupils from the straightforward pleasures of tales of action, through the interest of anecdotes from other people's lives, to the unspoken story surrounding a moment's perception. With each poem the focus of activity is participation in a story. The emphasis on story as against other elements in the poem can tempt vaguely coasting imaginations into focused activity.

Ballads are successful with younger classes. It is not difficult to involve twelve-year-olds in the performance of a ballad if the clear object is their activity, and not discussion of how a certain kind of poem works (see chapter 3). Performance of a ballad suggests creating a new ballad. Ballads with plenty of repetition in which the story-line is carried in two- or three-line stanzas are an easily imitated model. Traditional ballads should not be given a special textbook status but mixed with modern folk-ballads. With pupils concerned about their adult image it is sometimes better to use only modern folk-ballads which the pupils themselves suggest, and try arranging a spoken performance against the musical accompaniment.

Another experiment is to use the text of a ballad, old or new, unfamiliar to the class. What singer or group would make a good job of performing it? What sort of accompaniment does it need? Does it need editing to make it a hit?

Working on ballads is usually popular, which brings its own problem – how to persuade the game-players to leave the game. Looking for material for making a new ballad can become a way out from the folk ballad to the modern literary ballad. Set the class looking for material in the surrounding world, perhaps newspapers, TV, a 'true' story someone has heard, a local event. A group-exercise is how the material might be turned into a ballad. With some classes it is worth trying a stiffer challenge. Different groups are given charge of different sections of the story. The result of this is an awkward, ill-matched patchwork in which the point of the story wanders vaguely. This brings attention to the need for pattern. Examples of modern literary ballads show how pattern serves the point the ballad wants to make. The word 'examples' does not mean that one plans a lesson on technique: presentation aims at causing interest in the story. There is no need to *explain* that a story is an effective way of making people see the point. When their interest is caught, pupils do see the point. What follows is talk that goes out from the ballad to the pupils' own notions about the point seen. For example, *The Ballad of Rudolph Reed* (Gwendolyn Brooks) starts up discussion about cruelty or injustice or anger or family loyalty or violence.

The next stage is to try out poems which tell a quieter kind of story—stories which belong in the common light of day. There is a wide range of material in modern work, from poems whose narrative content is immediately striking, such as Frost's *Out, out . . .*, to poems which find a story in a simple encounter, such as Hewitt's *Turf-carrier on Aranmore*. If the emphasis of presentation is on the story, there is no need to confine choice to simple poems. In presentation, the important thing is to be a story-teller. Pupils should not see the text. What one exploits is the fact that listening-age is always much in advance of reading-age. A good reading can carry attention over difficulties of expression to understanding. Strategies like those used for prose fiction help to increase participation – role-playing, close-ups of a particular moment, seeing the story, planning a film version or a strip-cartoon version. But there is much to be said for often simply being a story-teller.

Stories of uncommon light—poems which use the mode of dream—are less certain of appeal. They do not always work with pupils who demand that all sense should be common. It is worth trying the effect of a poem of this kind and postponing further examples if this is rejected. *I started early, took my dog* (Dickinson) and *The Combat* (Muir) are good test-poems. The 'logic' of the telling may catch the imagination. If it does, the way is open for trying other examples. This kind of poem usually leads to curiosity about the meaning. In the search for the meaning all suggestions are given equal respect. (See also chapter 3.) The approach suggested earlier in the section *A shape for feeling* is helpful in this matter.

The last stage is the story contained in poems which don't appear to be telling a story at all: very short poems, traditional verse, haiku, epitaphs, humorous rhymes. These are treated as springboards for the pupils' inventive activity in oral story-telling. The 'plot' is identified. Then it expands backwards and forwards; the story-teller acquires a personality; distant characters come close; a place comes into focus; fragments of conversation are overheard. Another experiment reverses the process. A poem or short story already familiar to the class is reduced to a few lines.

Documents plus

This approach is based on the power of art to give a moment of human history permanent life, so that when it is come upon at a later time, the time-gap disappears. What is involved is recognition of the 'plus' of the poem as a record of human experience; a document in which facts breathe so that the reader can share in other lives. An advantage of the approach is its adaptability to the sophistication and imaginative reach of a particular class.

Behind the news

As a preliminary activity, the class tries humanizing documents, focusing on the people behind a news item, an excerpt from a report, facts in a survey. The work resembles that kind of writing exercise where the pupils act as reporters looking for the human interest in a story, but the emphasis is on the new data rather than the story. All that is required is that telling details should be invented; the story need not be written up. For example, say that the document is the latest unemployment figures. A person who has no job is created, and given a background. Then the character is caught at a particular moment, which shows him being affected—seeing the news item, shopping, waking in the morning. Attention is on what is happening now at this moment, not on what happens next as in a story. What details make the watcher share the character's knowledge? Gesture, posture, item of clothing, surroundings.

Excavation 2080AD

The class becomes a team of archaeologists a hundred years hence, examining a document find belonging to the 1980s. The teacher provides the data: commercial advertisements, pieces torn from popular magazines, bits of a survey, headlines from a newspaper, letters to the editor, a page from a sociologist's report; and a few poems about people written by living poets. The archaeologists' job is to 'read' the data in order to build a picture of the society represented there. The teacher helps in arranging the method of reporting and solving problems of comprehension, but does not try to impose a reading beyond the team's level of critical reflection.

The next experiment is to lay down a new deposit. This time the material is a pool of poems which the pupils select from those which they judge will carry forward most vividly what it is to be alive today. They add to the deposit examples of their own work and the lyrics of favourite songs.

Excavation 1980AD

For this dig the material is poetry from other times. The selection is miscellaneous in theme and time. Dating is not important; for many pupils their grandparents' youth as well as Blake's is the past. Chaucer can rub shoulders with Clare; Arthur Waley's translation of Chinese poems can be set beside Wilfred Owen's war poems. Choice is based on the reading agility of the class. Pupils are invited to suggest poems encountered in previous activities. Reading the data is a matter of finding a foothold in another world. Instructions to fieldworkers would run like this: Collect the details which distinguish the world of the poem from today's world. Are any of these so worn by time that you can't see clearly? What details belong to both worlds? Where do you catch the tone of the speaker's voice? Where do you know most surely what he is feeling? Findings are recorded briefly, the whole class working together or in small groups.

'The picture of nobody'

Strategies so far described involve the activity of the group. There still remains the challenge of the poem to the individual, the fact that the drama of the poem is frequently addressed to an audience of one. The challenge cannot easily be met until a fair quantity of poetry has been admitted to the classroom community, and there are signs of lessening hostility. The aim is to make room for private activity, for freeing the individual from the strong influence of group opinion.

Diary of Anon

A preliminary exercise seeks to awaken interest in a poem as a way of overhearing another's thinking and feeling. I suggest Anon for this step because he carries no implication of superior status, no threat of singularity. Anon might be anyone. The aim is implicit reinforcement of the fact that a poem grows out of someone's alertness to the day everyone lives in. The teacher provides a number of short poems by Anon; these include pieces already met as well as new pieces. Working orally, the class tries to go behind two or three of these to their source in Anon's experience. Say that Anon kept a diary: how might he have noted the idea, the event there? Entries are short, in note form. For example: *The Twa Corbies*—Cold today. Bitter wind. Saw two crows when out walking. Ugly creatures with their wicked beaks. Weird squawking. Always make me think of death. *Sauce for the Goose* —Another argument with the wife about smoking. Settled it by making fun of her new crinoline. Then each pupil chooses a few pieces and makes corresponding diary entries.

A possible follow-up for pupils who have been pleased with their own efforts at verse is to make an anthology called *More Poems by Anon.* Pupils are invited to submit contributions from their own work; each contribution is accompanied by a gloss, which could be a diary-entry or an early draft of the piece. Then some poems by poets other than Anon which have worked well are taken up again. The poems to choose are poems of the private world, poems, in fact, which address an audience of one, or no audience at all. Pupils select two or three for which they make diary entries. The aim of the exercise is to keep attention on making contact with another mind in action, and to reassure pupils about the adequacy of their understanding.

Anthology: 'I am'

Anthology making is always better if it has a definite focus which calls the critical faculty into play. One needs to forestall the random and partial attention which so often marks choice in this work. The starting-point is a poem strongly marked by the sense of self, of individual particularity. For older classes, Clare's *I am—yet what I am none cares or knows* is excellent; for younger classes, Dickinson's *I'm nobody —who are you?* Some other possibilities for older classes: *I cannot grow* (Auden), *Desert Places* (Frost), *I am afraid to own a body* (Dickinson); for younger classes, *The Father's Song* (Anon), *A Boy's Head* (Holub), *What is he?* (Lawrence). Discussion of the starting poem makes clear the focus of the anthology to be made—an anthology which speaks for the individual, the 'I', the unique private experience.

Each pupil becomes an editor selecting material for an anthology called *I am* or *The Picture of Nobody*. The main source is a stock of poems provided by the teacher. Editors are free to use other sources and to draw on poems met previously. The size of the anthology is adapted to the particular situation. As a general rule, the number of poems to be chosen is left open; or the teacher may decide to specify a minimum and maximum number, depending on the interest the work creates. One advantage of not specifying size is that it is easy to abandon the experiment if it goes flat.

An important feature of the anthology is that is has an appendix for 'Rejection Slips'. Here an editor enters those poems which he finds irritating, dull, false. The freedom not only to select but to declare rejection is a stimulus to reading. Of course, there are always pupils who appear to give all their energy to the Appendix. This is not something to worry about; active rejection is a form of recognition.

How selections are recorded is left to the pupils. Younger pupils whose interest is caught usually choose to make a book of their selection, either individual books or a single book to which all contribute. Older pupils seldom choose this labour. Some do transcribe their selection; some use a mixture of titles, complete poems, extracts; some add editorial comments, particularly in the Appendix; some merely list titles. It is worth making one stipulation in the matter of recording: that there should be a deliberate arrangement of material on a principle decided by the editor.

The results of the work are often surprising and encouraging, though one needs to be prepared for apparent failure. Again, it would be unwise to take individual anthologies as an infallible guide. When the exercise really does stir attention, there are always hints of a good deal of masking, particularly among older pupils. The real selection may be in the Appendix, not in the Anthology proper.

Listening in to the world

In this section I have in mind academically competent pupils who like their learning to be 'all very tidy'; pupils who have no difficulty in 'making good progress' and achieving the exam grade they aim at. They may have no objection to being taught poetry as long as they are also taught what examiners expect them to do with the stuff. The trouble is that growth and progress are not the same thing. Competence is no more a sign of a wakened imagination than indifference —and less than active rebellion. To be silenced by the silence of the poem, to be cut by the fine edge of language, is just as important for school volunteers as for school conscripts.

That poetry is a way of listening in to the world is the emphasis I should choose in this situation. What we want to happen is that intelligence should be moved as well as interested, should step past the fascination of contemporary knowledge to unheard questions of perennial human concern. The young people I am thinking of are interested in public issues, have opinions about them, and like talking about them. The poetry likely to start attention into life is poetry which explores such issues. The point of contact is the shared interest. What follows is again activity—the activity of discussion, not of the poem as a poem, but of the ideas it generates in the listeners. Poems are chosen as disturbers of the peace, challengers of conventional wisdom, 'but' *sayers*.

Modern Russian poetry is a rich place to start. The public importance of the poet in Russia challenges the notion that poetry is all right in its place, but that it hasn't much to do with really important things. The stories of Akhmatova, Pasternak, Mandel'shtam, Brodski provoke a revision of attitude to the profession of poetry. Start with the story of Osip Mandel'shtam—the years of persecution, the satire on Stalin, his obscure death in some prison-camp. Or start with a transcript of the trial of Joseph Brodski. Or the woman in the prison-queue asking Akhmatova, 'Can you describe this?'(**39**) Material like this leads naturally to discussion of a range of ideas: freedom of thought and speech, the pull between private and public good, boundaries of power, love of country. The poets themselves share in the discussion; some of their work is read so that they are present as invisible but audible participants.

'Listening in' begins in one country and spreads out across the world. The ideas generated by the Russian poets are followed elsewhere; the signals are picked up in different areas. In other approaches described in this chapter, the provenance of a poem is irrelevant; in this approach, the provenance is part of the activity. The teacher draws on a selection of poems from different countries which bring the listeners up against the interaction of the public and private worlds: war, famine, political and social injustice, economic inequality, the nuclear threat. On the whole, the poems come from the modern world, but it is worth taking sometimes a dive into the past. I should certainly try Blake's *London* ('I wander thro'each charter'd street') and Villon's *Ballade* ('So much the goat scratches he can't sleep'). Whether a poem is given a hearing depends on the direction discussion takes. It is best, I think, not to try to follow a straight line through a planned set of themes, but to keep open the possibility of unexpected juxtapositions. Destruction has several faces, thus Anthony Hecht's *More Light! More Light!* might enter the debate beside Muir's *Sick Caliban*; Cesar Vallejo's *Masses* beside Mary Gilmore's *Nationality* and Holub's *History Lesson*.

The work satisfies because it respects the pupils' own estimation of their maturity. There is another extremely important advantage. *So much you cry Noël that it comes*, says Villon. Against the babble of chaos, (many young people are very aware of the nuclear threat), poetry gives witness to human stability, not by ignoring the danger, but by finding its stubborn human scale. It speaks for the individual lives the statistics conceal.

3
'Children, if you dare to think'

(Robert Graves)

The question that concerns us in this chapter is how to quicken interest in the poem itself, to bring about the kind of direct confrontation which makes possible the clearing of imaginative sight that may occur in the experience of art. 'The perception of art,' says Vigotsky, 'requires creativity: it is not enough to experience sincerely the feeling, or feelings, of the author; it is not enough to understand the structure of the work of art; one must also creatively overcome one's own feelings and find one's own catharsis; only then will the effect of art be complete'(2). We cannot complete the effect of art for our pupils, but we can, I think, in our role as mediators, open or close the way for them to find the completion.

What is of great importance is that the way we present poetry sets the right area of the mind to work, makes space for the poem to do what it can do supremely, namely to call the intuitive and imaginative powers into action. Thus we do not distract young readers by trying to get poetry into line with other objects of study, presenting it as a problem to be solved. We try not to set up obstacles to the possibility of a creative dialogue, emptying out, for example, what Herbert Read calls 'the bag of monkey-tricks of English poetry', treating the poem as a collection of curious devices with unfamiliar names, many of them Greek. We keep lit.crit. out of the way. The job now is not the business of examining the elements of the poet's craft, but of establishing firmly the habit of sharing in the experience the craft makes possible. The way we work aims at strengthening the pupils' confidence in their native ability to recognize and enjoy what is going on in a poem. Underlying the approach is the reassurance that any reader brings a great deal to a poem, and that what he brings is essential to the experience.

Using anthologies

The more generous the supply of poetry available in the classroom the better. A single short anthology cannot really allow for diversity of taste, and when such a book is being used as the main source of choice, it is wise to have to hand supplementary material: a number of anthologies which are different from one another, in format and illustration, in thinness and fatness, in principles of selection and arrangement, conventional commercial editions as well as school editions (see appendix). For older classes there should be some books by individual poets. A further source is poems the teacher has come across elsewhere; a poem not in the available anthologies helps to break the connecting of poetry with what happens in school. Plenty of material means that an unpublished anthology which reflects the taste of a particular group of readers can grow in the course of a year; an anthology which contains far more poems than those which become the matter of an actual poetry lesson.

Which poems become the matter of poetry lessons, how many, and when they should be introduced, no outsider can decide. One takes direction always from the curiously unique identity of the class. A few principles would probably meet with general agreement: that it is better not to timetable poetry on a regular It's-Tuesday-so-it's-poetry basis; that the teacher is unlikely to waken interest in a poem which leaves him cold; that it is wise to abandon an intended lesson if the class is in an uncooperative mood; that poems should be chosen for their appeal to young readers rather than for their established reputation; that what a poem is concerned with and the kind of language used should not be remote from the pupils' experience. However, these principles are not beyond debate. A poem may turn restlessness into attentiveness. The past can come close because of a poem. A teacher's dislike may be challenged by the class. This has happened to me with—of all poems—Gray's *Elegy* and non-academic fourteen-year-olds. The success of Hopkins in the most unpromising situations turns upside down preconceptions about difficulty and relevance.

To keep the selection open, the class shares in deciding what poems are to become the matter of poetry lessons. Each member is asked to choose two or three poems from the available resources. The teacher chooses other poems to match these, contrast with them, take a theme further, bring his own predilections into play, and make sure that there is enough variety and challenge. The list that results will contain from fifty to a hundred poems. It remains open throughout the year for additions and subtractions. All the poems on a list will not become the subject of formal poetry work; the only condition is that everyone's choice is represented. The process of selection does not stop at the list, but operates within the poetry lesson itself. For instance, a lesson will frequently look at three or four poems together. All of these may remain at the forefront of attention, or one may push the others aside, perhaps to be taken up again in a later lesson, perhaps not.

Again, the rhythm of formal poetry lessons should, I think, vary: sometimes there will be stretches when no formal work is done; sometimes there will be a series of lessons centred on poetry.

What happens in a poetry lesson

What happens varies according to the poem, the class, the teacher. The approach aims at reflecting the fact that there are a number of ways of entering into a dialogue with a work of art. Variety is essential if interest is to be kept alive. Regular application of an all-purpose grid is a sad inhibitor of real collaboration. For instance, if what always happens is that the poem is discussed stanza by stanza, attention quickly slides back from the particular event. A prime virtue of the work of art is its power to surprise us into personal activity. Routine gets in the way of surprise; stands in the poem's light.

When reading a poem we intend to put before a class, we read in two ways. We read as adults who bring to collaboration independent experience of many poems, and of living. We are aware of the complex activity going on, and open to new recognitions, however familiar we are with the poem. We read also as mediators of the poem to an inexperienced audience who will not hear as we do. In this role we look to the poem itself to suggest a foothold, a way of enabling particular new readers to participate in the event. The richer the poem, the greater the number of possible points of contact, but any poem worth its place in the classroom will offer some choice of foothold.

The strategies suggested in chapter 2 involve preparatory activity before the poems themselves are encountered. Some teachers would hold that this should always be the way, that 'a poem must be seen as an end rather than as a beginning'(**17**). Certainly, the approach to any poem involves preparing the class to receive it, but the amount and degree vary as much as the poems themselves. Preparation ranges from simply making sure that the class is ready to listen, to detailed exploration of the children's experience of the poem's concerns. The kind of preamble necessary is decided in the light of the poem and the particular class. The question to ask oneself is: how much am I needed in this meeting of imaginations? Again, a poem may be not an end, but a more effective beginning than anything I can think of. One advantage of presenting a few poems together is that a poem can sometimes do the job for us: a poem that needs no preamble can open the way to a more demanding poem which might otherwise need too much preliminary comment.

It would hardly need saying that the preamble should be worthy of the poem if inappropriate preamble were not so common among student-teachers. It may be wise to investigate the children's idea of bats before reading Lawrence's *Man and Bat*. But a chat about the zoo is not the way to get a class into the right mood for Blake's *Tyger*, a poem well able to look after its own introduction, whatever the level of the class. A copy of Breughel's *Icarus* is proper company for William Carlos Williams' *Landscape with the Fall of Icarus*, since the poem grows directly from the painting, but a plate of mushrooms does nothing to lead a class into the subtle life of Sylvia Plath's *Mushrooms*. Visual aids, even good ones, are most often an irrelevant distraction. When the poem itself is a picture, the so-called aid prevents the receiving imagination from re-composing its own picture from the poem.

An anxious practice from which student-teachers need to be saved is that of starting by abstracting the hard words and explaining them, a practice which ensures that the class is on track for a completely different kind of learning from that intended. Poetic words live and breathe in the structure of the poem. Their activity is paralysed if they are first encountered as if their natural habitat was the dictionary. Another way of cluttering access is to introduce the poet rather than the poem, handing out a few scraps of biographical information. Sometimes a poet's life is a valuable point of contact, but mostly it is irrelevant now. Let the listeners have the poem clean, respecting the value of the innocent ear, which means that pupils can encounter a work without the prejudice of fashionable or acquired literary opinion.

Collaboration with a poem is our concern in the rest of this chapter. The guiding principle is that a poem is an event which can be shared, and which is understood in the sharing. For the adolescent the sense of understanding is an essential part of the enjoyment. He wants to feel that he knows what is going on. He is very much closer to the adult reader in his way of responding now than he is to his younger self. He would agree with W. K. Wimsatt's starting-point: 'At the outset what can we be sure of? Mainly that a poem says or means something, or ought to mean something'(**18**). Continuing interest depends upon the desire for meaning being satisfied; confidence grows with repeated experience of his own capacity to understand.

Finding a foothold of meaning in a poem is not a matter of paraphrase, of synonyms, of reducing it to other terms, but of sharing as deeply as possible in the event. Poetic meaning is come upon in the act of participation. In the classroom the meaning is not the whole complex of meaning of a poem, but such meaning as is within the reach of given readers. We try to help the young reader to take what he can, which is, I believe, very much more than he can articulate, as it is with all of us. What we want him to discover now is the pleasure of being dared into thinking and feeling:

> 'Children, if you dare to think
> Of the greatness, rareness, muchness,
> Fewness of this precious only
> Endless world in which you say
> You live . . .'
> *Warning to Children*   (Robert Graves)

The skill of listening

'Read it with the ears', said Hopkins, 'and my verse becomes alright'(**19**). The part that the eye plays in knowing what is going on in drama, the ear plays in knowing what is going on in poetry. What Hopkins calls 'the figures of sound' are a vital element in the poem's passing from page to imagination; the skill of listening is indispensable to understanding. For the experienced reader, the attention of the ear is automatic when he reads a poem silently. It is not automatic for the inexperienced reader, and its becoming so depends on acquiring the habit of 'reading with the ears'. There is one fact we need to keep in mind in this connection. A great deal of the reading a secondary pupil does across the curriculum demands the ability to read with the eye, not the ear, and much energy is naturally given to helping pupils to increase their skill in rapid eye-reading. But this skill is useless for reading poetry. It is impossible to skim a poem. The organization of language there demands the slower attention of the ear, an attention learned through hearing poetry read aloud.

So the first step is always the teacher reading the poem as a whole and the pupils listening. The practice of listening without looking develops the habit of attending to those all-important 'figures of sound'. It is commonly recommended that a second reading aloud should follow immediately on the first. This gives time for attention to gather round the event now present. In the second reading the teacher is sensitive to the effect of the first reading, and in the light of this may make slight shifts in emphasis to reinforce the effect or to bring something new to the foreground. A change in pace, an emphasized rhythm can prevent the second reading from becoming a routine affair rather than a practice which heightens attentiveness.

The habit of reading with the ear is reinforced by the pupils' own reading aloud, but this is practicable only for a short time in the secondary school. Once self-consciousness takes over and pupils begin to be embarrassed by the sound of their own voices, to insist that they read poetry aloud is damaging rather than helpful. It is worth making it a fairly regular practice while the children are still at ease with it. The ease can disappear very quickly and it is wise to seize the opportunity in the first year where reading aloud is usually popular.

Direct vocal collaboration is invited with poems of strong rhythmic pattern. The natural way of taking possession of such poems is to join in the rhythmic play. Ballads are an obvious example. Various renderings are tried out: trying the effect of different voices for different characters, of groups of different size for narrative links, the whole group for the refrain, a single voice for repeated phrases or the moment of crisis; trying the effect of a pause, of a change of pace or tone. There is seldom any need for resuming the story. By the end of the exercise, everyone knows it. If individual variations appear, so much the better. That is in the true ballad tradition. It does not take a class long to become adept at this kind of play, and it is an excellent means of helping pupils whose sense of rhythm is poor.

There is a more sophisticated kind of vocal exploration which is enormously valuable in teaching implicitly the relationship between sound and meaning. What I have in mind is poems at the other end of the rhythmic scale, where the mode is 'to compose in sequence of the musical phrase, not in sequence of the metronome'(20). Christopher Smart's *For I will consider my cat Jeoffrey* is an early example. After the teacher's reading, the class breaks into small groups each of which is responsible for working out a reading of a certain section of the poem. It is important not to get in the way: explanation is given only when it is asked for. All sorts of subtleties emerge through testing the heard movement of the piece, which no amount of paraphrase of what-the-poet-says can achieve. The work ends with the children's reading, not with an attempt to wrap up meaning.

Lawrence's *Snake* is a marvellous example of how a poem makes itself clear in the hearing. The argument between instinct and reason reaches understanding as the ear picks up the snake-like movement; now flowing, now flickering, now slack, frequently turning back on itself. A first hearing leads to recognition of the two voices in the poem: the narrative voice which carries the visible event and the reflecting voice which carries the watcher's reactions to the event. This suggests trying a two-voice reading, with the class working in pairs. It is easy for the children to decide which voice different lines belong to. What sharpens attention as they prepare a reading is to tell them to watch for the clear directions in line and phrase as to pacing. The instruction controls the urge to impose the wrong kind of drama.

Older classes, past the stage of reading aloud themselves, can be taken further into the activity of *Snake* through attention to the play of voice. They can come to the recognition that there are more than two voices at work. The word *voice* occurs first in line 22. Is there silence —inner and outer—before that? What happens when *the voice of my education* gives place to *voices in me* two lines later? Try naming the different voices that enter the debate at this point and work with and against the voice of education. Where do these voices become part of the visible event rather than a reflection on it from outside? What voice/voices do the repetitions belong to? What happens in the line 'I despised myself and the voices of my accursed human education?' Trace that note *my* back through the poem and forward to the last occurrence, *my snake*. What voice is speaking in the last six lines? The purpose is to keep attention on how much the poem asks to be heard. Understanding is less likely to stick at the level of seeing the guilt and shame as simply the result of education.

Such exploration would not of course work with all classes. The subtlety of Lawrence's play with the word *my*, for instance, would not mean much to pupils whose conceptual activity is immature. In that case I should concentrate on the rich visibility of the event and what the speaker is feeling at different stages. The important thing is that there would be frequent relistening. As attention is drawn to certain lines, the lines are read aloud, not just looked at.

Mushrooms (Sylvia Plath) makes an exhilarating experiment in listening for any class. Record the poem in a stage-whisper, play it to the class and see what happens. After the first explosion of curiosity, pleasure, irritation, try a few more replayings, matching each with a specific focus of attention. This time ignore the meaning of the words and pick up the pattern of sound only. What echoes settle in the ear? Does the thing rhyme? This time find the sort of meaning that is going on: fast, slow, regular, jerky? Or is there movement at all? This time let the sense of touch work. Feel out the contours—curved or angled; the surface—smooth or rough; the weight—light or heavy? Watch the speakers—*so many of us*. What sort of shape, colour, gesture? What picture forms in the listeners mind? Comfortable, uncomfortable? Finally, read the poem at normal pitch, giving the title.

Explicit attention to the figures of sound is not always profitable or practicable at this stage. Indeed, with many poems the sound remains an implicit part of the experience. We trust the impact rather than investigate the effect. The question, 'What is the effect?' is one to use sparingly, for it may distract attention rather than focus it. It is a right question when raised by the pupils themselves. For example, when a third year group were talking about *Fear no more the heat of the sun* (Shakespeare), one pupil said that although the poet kept repeating *Fear no more*, the feeling you got was one of fear. Another suggested that the reason was the other repeated words: *all, must, come to dust,* which make you afraid for yourself. If the teacher had asked, 'What is the effect of the repetitions?' it is unlikely that this perception would have occurred at all. Taking direction from the response of the class is a matter of waiting for them to give us the go-ahead sign. When the form of a poem is unusual, this is often the first signal the pupils seize on. This happens with Hopkins and Dylan Thomas. A common response to *And death shall have no dominion* is the desire to hear it again—and again. e.e. cummings is another poet who tempts the ear. What is happening in *anyone lived in a pretty how town* always begins with the oddity of expression. Usually it works well to attend first to the play with *anyone, no one, someones, everyones*. Once *anyone* and *no one* are recognized to be 'he' and 'she', the biography falls into place and other oddities stimulate ingenuity rather than dismay.

A very different example of how sound can be drawn into exploration of meaning at this stage is *The Bird* (George MacBeth). In this piece there is no oddity; it moves straight and plain. The teacher's first reading obeys meticulously the two-stress phrasing, the five-line stanza. After the first reading the event is clear: a man finds a bird half-dead on the kitchen floor; he strikes it with a broom four times

until it is dead, lifts it on to a shovel, tips it into the dustbin. That is
what is seen. What is known? Before the second reading, invite the class
to let the pacing speak as well as the details. What is happening besides
the visible event? What words or lines strike the ear? What the pupils
notice in the second listening takes exploration into the thinking and
feeling that accompanies each step. For example, the killing:

> By the handle near to
> The head and struck
> The bird four times.

What words does the pacing cause to stand out here? In the third
stanza while the bird is still alive: *I picked it up*. In the seventh:

> I edged the remains
> Up with a red
> Plastic shovel

Is there a different meaning of *up* in the lines? If you place *I carried it out*
against *I tipped it out*, has *out* quite the same meaning in each line?
Listening to the deliberate pacing can lead to a further perception with
an alert class. The setting of the small event—an ordinary house—is
given harsh contrasting weight through the line-arrangement. How
often do details of setting mark the end of a line? Now listen to the final
stanza. What is the speaker recognizing there?

'My words echo thus in your mind' (**21**). The skill of listening is
developed through the echo always being a major part of what goes on.
With junior classes at least the skill can be agreeably reinforced in a
festival of listening, perhaps a radio programme assembled, arranged
and read by the pupils. The aim would be to reflect the great variety of
pleasure for the ear available in poetry, from *Edward, Edward* to *I sing of
a maiden*; from *Macavity* (Eliot) to *The Cow* (Ogden Nash); from
Ploughing on Sunday (Wallace Stevens) to *The Gallows* (Edward
Thomas); from *Upon the Snail* (Bunyan) to *French Persian Cats* (Edwin
Morgan), and so on, and so on. For older pupils the skill is further
developed through critical listening to recordings of poems they know
and like. It is best to use more than one recording of a piece. All
recordings should not be professional, and accents should not be uni-
formly standard. There are usually pupils willing to make anonymous
recordings; friends too can be pressed into service.

The question of questioning

Openness about the kind of thinking started up in the classroom is
essential, not only because of the subjective appeal of the work of art,
but also because subjectivity of response is natural to the young mind.
While pupils are still at the stage of wanting to make a poem fit

themselves, there is little to be gained from trying to force an ability to examine a poem objectively. It should not worry us, for instance, if a junior class treats the poem as a diving-board for jumping on and off. Poems which are obviously related to the pupils' everyday world may cause them to speed away from the poem itself to talking about their own knowledge of a similar event. This can happen at any level and is always right when it does. Putting one's own experience beside the experience of the poet is a critical act, however elementary. If the poem is turned to again at the end of the period, there is a much heightened awareness because of what has happened in between.

Questioning aims at taking the class past the primary pleasure into closer dialogue with what has caused the pleasure, at strengthening the hold of imagination and feeling on the poem. The aim is not that the children should be able to achieve the impossible task of paraphrase. Questions are successful when they lead towards a further question —the question the poem itself is asking, which may not be the same for every reader. Sometimes the final question may be just that: What question is the poem asking? If it results in a variety of answers, so much the better. Again, it is always a sign of true engagement if our questions prompt questions rather than answers. The point is that what is important is not that the class should guess what we are thinking, but that they should discover what they themselves are thinking. That is why the question-grid approach is unsatisfactory: it implies that there is a corresponding answer-grid. If a book is being used which offers a set of questions for each poem, it is essential to examine their appropriateness in the light of the children we know, and to select only those likely to strike fire. We are not teaching strangers. Censoring is necessary for the questions we ourselves make out. It is wise to examine these for a tendency to ask the same kind of question on any poem; it is also well to keep in mind that we are experienced adults whose habits of analysis may hamper our seeing as our pupils can see. Further, we need to be ready to abandon a line of questioning altogether if response takes off in a different direction.

Every poem, plain or coloured, is a metaphor. The paradox of the metaphor, both in the narrow sense of the individual figure and in the wider sense of the poem as a whole, is that it acts literally before it acts non-literally. Poets, in Marianne Moore's words, are 'literalists of the imagination'(**22**). For our purposes, that 'literalism' is of prime importance. The thinking the poem stirs is the result of participation which has nothing to do with trying to understand the concept 'metaphor'. *On First Looking into Chapman's Homer* illustrates the point. When Keats says 'Much have I travelled in the realms of gold' the voyage is literal. For any reader, participation in the metaphor begins and in a sense ends there, for it is the way the poem goes beyond the particular of the poet's experience into the experience of astronomer and sailor. For the experienced reader, Chapman, Homer, Apollo, Cortez form their double relations as he reads, but for the inexperienced reader, the relations remain single, as names in a golden voyage. If we begin with the question, 'Does anyone know who Homer was?' or the information that Chapman translated the work of the Greek poet Homer, the all-important voyage is in danger of slipping out of sight, and participation in the metaphor at best weakens, at worst ceases. Pupils may learn that Keats is talking about reading books, and that he compares his reading to the experience of an astronomer and a discoverer. But they have the wrong scrap of the metaphor in their hands. Information has taken precedence over 'seeing feelingly'. To increase participation in the metaphor, we should instead aim first at strengthening their first true recognition of the voyage. The title is best omitted altogether: for young readers it is an unpromising linguistic puzzle.

What do the children see as they listen—ignoring for the moment the bits they don't understand? A pooling of sight yields realms, states and kingdoms, coming at last to a new island where Homer is king; an astronomer discovering a new star, an explorer called Cortez with his men staring silently at the ocean from a mountain-top (this last after a break for amusement at the word *stout*). If this is followed by identifying the feeling that grows in the poem, readers seldom miss the quietness of wonder in the first part and the quickening of excitement in the second. It is when the relations have been seen like this that one can move safely to the double relations, to explaining who Homer and Chapman are, and Apollo's connection with poetry. The result is often a thrill analogous to Keats's, as the real question of the poem itself is recognized: the sudden sun of understanding what it means to be surprised by something wonderful seen for the first time.

The point is that questioning proceeds from the known to the unknown. What is known is the event the reading has made present, vaguely or vividly, in the children's minds. Every poem is approached as an event which invites participation. Questioning always starts not with difficulties but with certainties, seeks always to strengthen trust in the validity of what is seen unaided. The starting-point is, 'What is happening here and now?' For any reader at any level of sophistication, engagement with a new poem begins in picking up those signals which are clear to him. For us, it is important to remember that the poem is new to the pupils. We need to keep our familiarity with it out of the way, to be sensitive to what the innocent ear takes hold of first. 'What is happening?' invites a coming close to the event and keeps attention on the presentness. Since it focuses on what all can see, it counters the tendency to think in terms of right and wrong answers. Most importantly, it has the effect of shifting the activity of questioning from teacher to pupils. The process of understanding follows the order their interest dictates, which is seldom a stanza-by-stanza order.

> The maidens came
> When I was in my mother's bower.
> I had all that I would.
>> The bailey beareth the bell away;
>> The lily, the rose, the rose I lay.
>
> The silver is white, red is the gold;
> The robes they lay in fold.
>> The bailey beareth the bell away;
>> The lily, the rose, the rose I lay.
>
> And through the glass window shines the sun.
> How should I love and I so young?
>> The bailey beareth the bell away;
>> The lily, the rose, the rose I lay.

The first signal of the event to be seized on (by younger pupils) is almost always that in the last stanza:

> How should I love and I so young?

'It's a girl going to be married—it's the morning of the day and she's glad because the sun is shining.' (Then the *maidens* in the first stanza are identified.) 'The bridesmaids are helping her to dress—her dress is laid out on the bed.' (Girls frequently take the second stanza as describing the dress.) 'Her dress is gold and silver—what's *lay in fold*?' (At this stage pupils see the event as clear, and appear not to think that the refrain needs explanation any more than the refrain in a ballad. Someone may say the bells are ringing. It is when the poem is read again to listen to the feeling coming through that the mysteriousness opens out. Now opinions begin to differ.) 'She's happy—She's excited—I think she's not sure —She's afraid —She think's she's too young—She's surprised that it's happening to her—What does *I had all that I would* mean?—Then she's not sure, she has everything she wants at home—But it could mean she has everything she wants *now*, for the wedding.' (At this point suggestions about the meaning of the silver and the gold might be canvassed.) Disagreement about the feeling causes the refrain to be drawn into the argument. 'What is she doing with the lily and the rose? Are they flowers for her bouquet?—What's a *bailey*? He's taking the bell *away*—It sounds more as if it was all over —Perhaps it never happened at all—Could she be mad?' The importance of the refrain in the impact is emphasized if the poem is now read without it. Then the refrain is listened to in isolation; different readings reveal the different movements possible in

> The lily, the rose, the rose I lay.

A lilt of happiness or a slow reflectiveness? Why *the rose* twice? Now it is time to hand the poem over to individual possession. It is read again and the listeners write down what they see as happening in it.

Portable drama

Think of a poem as a scrap of the world caught in action and given a place in language; portable drama which the imagination of the reader takes into stock by watching rather than by rote-learning. Any poem can be seen in this way. For young readers the ability is developed through poems which clearly invite attention to a brief drama.

The drama may be very simple, for example, *On Roofs of Terry Street* (Douglas Dunn). Someone in the street lifts his head and looks. Follow the moving camera of his eyes across the roofs. Something happens —*becomes precious*. Looking leads the writer to knowing—what? Try beside that a drama from centuries ago, *Pangur Bán*. A scholar and a cat at work. Is the writer's happy understanding out of date? Is there any connection with the Terry Street poem?

Or *A bird came down the walk* (Emily Dickinson). The stage is a garden path. Keep your eyes on the bird's movement. Has what is going on anything to do with us? The watcher moves and the bird disappears: what kind of movement now? Up to the last stanza, what is recorded is what is actually there before the writer's eyes. What sort of seeing happens when the bird has taken flight? Try standing back to watch the poet watching. What kind of thinking is going on? What about feeling?

Sometimes one might use the terms of drama, i.e. setting, scene, action, to keep attention focused. For example, take *Little Fable* (Roy Fuller) Scene I. Brightly lit room. Sudden movement. There it goes. How much of the room is visible as a result of the movement? The size of what happens, the watchers sensation. Scene 2. Now what size is the room? What is going on there? What has happened to feeling? Scene 3. From the *halting clockwork* movement of Scene I to what? Feeling now? Has there been a victory? What about the missing scene, the one played off-stage? Is there any sense in which it flashes on the reader's eye? What does the writer recognize in *feet formed properly*?

Frost's '*Out, Out, –*' presents for the private theatre drama of another depth. I should want a class to experience the gradual diminishment from a world of sense to *no more to build on there*. Attention after the first reading would follow that progress to bring about recognition of the narrowing focus. Let the first scene reveal its ordinary busy 'aliveness': noise, smell, late light, changing rhythm of the saw, sticks of wood—the satisfaction of it. How big is the world here? How big is it in the second scene, the scene of the accident? What has repetition of the word *hand* to do with how sight is compelled? *They*, *them* – how clear are the other actors? *They* and we see the details of the accident—or do we? Just what is seen? Who/what moves? *Rueful laugh*; *Then the boy saw all*—what gulf is fixed between boy and watchers? The third scene begins with the word *so* raised to the rank of a sentence. How much does the word contain? What has happened to the setting the poem begins with? Watch how death comes. The others at the moment? *No more to build on there.*

Connect this with *He saw all spoiled*. The kind of connection made helps to reveal the maturity of response occurring and is a guide to how much further to go. This is the moment, I think, for taking in the title '*Out, out – *': Macbeth, hearing of his wife's death and seeing a man's life as having no more strength than a candle flame—'Out, out, brief, candle . . .'. The poem is read again as a whole. Immature readers usually stop at the connection between *puffed his life out with his breath* and Macbeth's words. For them the last question might simply be to try to explain what they find saddest about the event. More mature readers, certainly if they know *Macbeth*, may perceive the irony in the allusion. Turn their attention to the mind that makes participation possible. What time do the lines *and nothing happened . . . saved from work* belong to? Where else does that other time enter the telling? What question about death does the whole poem turn on?

Portrait poems make eminently portable drama. 'A shilling life will give you all the facts', as Auden puts it (**23**). A poem cuts through the facts to the riddle of owning a life. Participation for the adolescent is not a matter of the uncritical total identification that occurs at an earlier stage. The imaginative projection that can occur now involves an acknowledgement of separateness; an important feature of response, for it is the way we learn to allow others their difference as well as recognize their kinship.

The underlying emphasis of exploration is always the interaction of two lives; that of the poem's subject and that of the reader. Thus, exploration is frequently followed by the pupils' trying their hand at creating portraits from their own experience. For example, *Aunt Julia* (Norman MacCaig), a portrait discovered in childhood memory, would lead to the readers rummaging in their own early memory for a parallel experience. Exploration of the poem shows them how to search. The rich oddity of Aunt Julia as the child saw and sensed her is there, whole and vivid, as if no time had intervened. So is the child's feeling for her and the remembering adult's feeling. Adolescents are far enough from their childhood to work out the difference between the two kinds of feeling, and to examine their own reader-response to Aunt Julia, which is different again. Examining their presence in the poem starts up interest in rediscovery of their own early way of seeing people.

What is he? (Lawrence) can set moving a wheel of thinking. Understanding of Lawrence's irritation with the questioner usually comes easily enough. There should be room for the objection: 'He is quibbling. It's all very well to say a man doesn't need a job.' Bring *The Diviner* (Heaney) into the argument. Here a man's gift of doing is not separated from his gift of being, but is given a name too. It is a good piece for participation in miniature drama. Find the gestures of the actor; find the line of contact between his body and what happens under the soil; be one of the bystanders. An uninhibited class might try miming the event. What would Lawrence say to Heaney, Heaney to Lawrence? Turn to some other job-poems, ordinary and extraordinary. Does the job get in the way of being a man? How much does it influence the outsider's view? Try the challenge of *A Civil Servant* (Graves). This starts with the satisfaction of joining in the mockery, in the pilgrims' *childlike merriment*. Then the 'but' of the portrait emerges. Plot the drama *down the years*, starting backwards from the last scene. Leave the pilgrims and join the speaker. What does the reader know that the pilgrims don't? Is mockery the whole story? *Not once was I aware—My rageless part*. Is job-hazard peculiar to civil servants only? Get Lawrence to act as guide to the pilgrims. Take in *Wings* (Miroslav Holub) and see what it has to contribute to the relation between working and living.

Participation in poems about people extends knowledge of the other, the stranger—and the stranger, of course, often lives next door. There is an immediate appeal in contemporary portraits, and most anthologies contain material both cheerful and pathetic. Poems which dare thinking about a world of neighbours are obviously valuable in the education of moral awareness. Related work would try to carry over the lesson of inimitability, of irreplaceable selfness. It is contemporary work, I think, which is most likely to jolt a young reader into realizing that he too is seen, is a 'portrait' for others.

But it would be a pity to confine the gallery to the present scene. Changes in society don't create a new human species and meeting themselves in the past extends understanding of continuing human specificity for young readers as for all of us. Chaucer certainly has his place for the unfaded sturdiness of life in his people and the clearsightedness of his moral response. One way of introducing portraits from the *Prologue* is to start with the fancy-dress, with illustrations of some of the pilgrims. How does the modern eye respond? What does it notice? Then let Chaucer take over and instruct seeing. With many classes it may be wise to use a modernized version to start with and follow this with the original version rendered in the accent scholars suggest might have been Chaucer's own (**24**). Pupils find the accent irresistible. The effect is to narrow the distance and increase the laughter. The details of the portrait spring to life: the Wyf of Bath's deafness, the Miller's wart, the Prioresse's dainty table manners, the Reeve's thinness, the Monk's polished surface. They inspire the creation of parallel portaits: popstar, heroine of a TV soap-opera, politician, teacher, hairdresser, footballer, computer expert, industrialist, trade-union official, bank manager, employment official, and so on.

Examining portrait poems involves examining the bundle of preoccupations, prejudices, preconceptions that complicates the way we see other people. Whether the habit of thinking again is carried over to actual experience is not something we can control, but at least the possibility has been created. Poems which attend to the lonely, the suffering, the left-outside, are valuable in the education of a generous imagination. Examples are *Telephone Conversation* (Wole Soyinka); *Ballad of Rudolph Reed* (Gwendolyn Brooks); *Home-burial* (Frost); *Sunday Afternoons* (Anthony Thwaite); *The Place's Fault* (Philip Hobsbaum); *My parents kept me from children who were rough* (Spender).

With such poems the moment of the character's history which the poem selects points to other moments which come to life in the reader's participation. The act of bringing them to life is a way of coming closer to the meaning. For example, *Sunday Afternoons* (Thwaite). The given drama is the poet's response to what he sees in the station buffet-bar. Collaboration begins in noticing what he makes present: the nothing-happening, the suspended action, the silence, the people *sitting thick as birds*, the room cut off behind *the fog thick on the glass*. In the centre of the poem comes the sound of a train shunting. Who hears the sound? Who is aware of the ghosts of other dramas: *saying goodbye*, *tears*, *promises to write*, *journeys*? *They know one another.* What kind of knowing is this? Within the given drama is the burden of dramas the poet cannot lift. The pupils are invited to select one of these and try to bring it to life, keeping in mind the given drama in which it begins. For example: *They exchange a few words*; *Waiting for the time to pass*; *Here there are other things to mull over*; *Thoughts of a place for the night*; *The night begins*.

'The whole experiment of green'

The quick curiosity of the senses, the unreflecting wonder of childhood response to the natural world fans out in a number of directions as head and heart grow. There is the pleasure or irritation of how sun or rain or birds or rats or daffodils or dandelions impinge on daily comfort. There is the habit of using nature as a common source of metaphor and analogy, so deeply part of language behaviour that we are hardly conscious of it. There is the rational satisfaction of the physical sciences, observing, classifying, analyzing natural phenomena. There is the aesthetic pleasure in natural forms, the surprise of a leaf in light, of the shapes of wind. There is the speculative fascination of the multiplicity and harmony of the 'tremendous scene' of which we are quantitatively so small a part.

Adolescents are at a stage between the unreflecting pleasure of the child and the reflecting satisfaction of the adult. Most perhaps have not the time or inclination to 'stand and stare'. But the original contact is part of their stock and ready for reflective exploration. The readiness shows in their own efforts at verse, even that of inveterately urban children who previously appeared hostile to 'all that nature rubbish'. They draw on natural phenomena to express feeling, often with a clumsy freshness which suggests that the reason goes deeper than received notions of what you should do in poetry. They are ready for thinking about human relationship with the natural world, for an examined response. In drawing the non-language world into 'the cool web of language'(**25**), poetry stimulates awareness of the different ways of human contact with that world. It offers the possibility of freeing the young imagination from the narrowness of the immediate physical environment, whether that is one of streets or of fields. The kind of poetry we choose is important. The essential quality is particularity, a sense of for-the-first-time-seen. It is this quality which makes the work of Clare, Hopkins, Frost, Emily Dickinson and Ted Hughes, so successful in the classroom. What happens, I suggest, is that the work of poets like these both reactivates earlier unquestioned pleasures of childhood and satisfies awakening discrimination. Wordsworth, for most pupils, is probably best left till later: his habit of looking back from the distance of maturity sets up an unpopular age-barrier. But there are exceptions—the Skating passage from the *Prelude*, for instance. Again, there is no need to confine oneself to material which the children can verify from their immediate environment. Film and television have greatly extended that environment, and the particularity of the poem deepens virtual experience of this wider environment in giving it the intimate permanence of language.

An obstacle to nature poetry causing enjoyment is a general invitation to admire the beauty of nature. What one watches for is the particular relationship a poem explores; one then takes direction from that.

The moral question of man kills beast seldom fails to stir interest. Attention begins in participating in the drama and goes on naturally to debating the rightness or wrongness. Does the poem come down on one side? Take *The Gallows* (Edward Thomas) for example. Response begins in sympathy, in sharing the sad flapping rhythms. But who is to blame for all the death? The keeper? Who sees the creatures as deserving death? A keeper keeps game—for what purpose? The question comes nearer home in poems which deal with the act of killing, where the poet's sense of guilt starts up the question of everyone's responsibility. Examples are *First Blood* (Jon Stallworthy); *Dawn Shoot* (Seamus Heaney); *The Image* (Roy Fuller); *The Wasps' Nest* (George Macbeth); *The Fox* (Clare). The effect is often unresolvable argument about any killing of creatures. It is not resolving the argument or counting heads on either side which matters, but the examining of the attitudes involved.

The to and fro of argument is not always the way. It is not, I think, the activity *Pheasant* (Sylvia Plath) should lead to. The poem asks for a letting be rather than the energy of debate. I should focus attention on what the poet discovers as she examines her thinking about the pheasant. What pictures of it does she *own* in her memory? Look at them. What new picture does her imagination create? Each picture is matched by a thought, an attempt to say why the bird matters to her. Read off the thoughts. *I trespass stupidly*. Where? Why stupidly? If the children know Lawrence's *Snake*, they will recognize the echoes in Plath's poem. Older pupils may go on to notice the differences and to discover in themselves a strong preference for one poem over the other.

One point about *Pheasant*. Can it work for children who have never seen a pheasant, even a picture of one? I think the answer is yes, but it is a case for preliminary stirring of the imagination. Not at first by showing a picture, but by evoking knowledge of wild birds they have all seen. Whatever the environment, it has plenty of birds. Get the children to examine their knowledge of how birds move on the ground. At this point a picture of a pheasant is useful but not essential. More stimulating is the teacher's account of seeing a pheasant.

A possible exercise to prompt thinking about this poem towards action: *It startles me still*. Select one memory-picture of a creature. Let it become clear. Look hard at it. What single detail about it most startles you still?

Clare's wonderful lucidity, that passion of unselfregarding attentiveness allows the reader to walk straight into a poem and be hardly aware he is listening to words. Clare not only instructs looking but also makes it possible for young readers to see a countryside they have no direct experience of. The picture-composition suggested in chapter 2 might now be followed by noticing the language that gives the reader the freedom of the event. Pupils are invited to locate the words without which the reader could not see so plainly. The invitation is deliberately specific: each pupil is asked to select just one word and one phrase; to try to find two moments where he sees as clearly as if he was John Clare. The difficulty of selection prevents casual attention. Individual choices usually show an interesting diversity and most of the poem can be reconstructed from putting them together. For example, *Mouse's Nest*: *progged* and *I ran and wondered*; *pushed* and *banging at her teats*; *craking* and *a ball of grass*; *bolted* and *glittered in the sun*; *stirred* and *the mouse hurried*. The aim is to get the readers to examine their own participation without the worry of having to explain a choice.

Clare gives easy access to the past. This can stir to life the perception of a living world that does not change as the human world changes. For older pupils an interesting way of bringing the perception to conscious reflection is to follow a group of Clare poems by *Hawk Roosting* (Ted Hughes). The difficulty of Hughes's poem is lessened if it is read in the light of Clare's work. What would Clare recognize in the poem? What would puzzle him? How might one explain to Clare what Hughes means by saying:

> It took the whole of Creation
> To produce my foot, my each feather.

Isolate the parts of the poem that stress the gulf between man and hawk. What would Clare have to say about the gulf? Start the two poets talking about the final stanza.

We cannot discourse to pupils about a sense of the particular, but we can help them to experience it at work in a poem and to discover the pleasure of sense, feeling and intelligence acting together. The number of things that meet and match joyfully in *Pied Beauty* (Hopkins), for example. Shake them apart, scatter the pieces: sky, cow, rose, mole, trout, coal, chestnuts, finches, tools. Now listen again and watch the pattern reforming. Or *A narrow fellow in the grass* (Dickinson). Not once the word *snake*. Instead, sudden noiseless movements so clearly named that we not only recognize the creature, but share the poet's *zero at the bone*. Or *Was Worm* (May Swenson). Again the butterfly is not given its common label, but instead is named in the particular way it has of being alive. Or *November* (Ted Hughes). For every detail of the common experience of winter rain and wind there is a new particular word.

A poem says: Look at these common things in this particular way. Collaboration begins there. It is important to give enough time for looking, enough time for the children to bring their memory stock into play beside the poet's. Hopkins provokes a riddle-solving activity; it is part of his appeal, perhaps, for young readers. What is valuable is that working out the riddle activates the reader's memory of related things. He discovers how much he knows. Unfamiliar words quickly become familiar in the process, for instance, *brinded* and *stipple* in *Pied Beauty*, because the context makes them visible as things. Understanding begins with things and moves from that to the thinking the things cause. For example, understanding *November* depends on participating in the density of sense-experience in the poem. Of the forty lines, only eleven are concerned with the tramp. Attention is first given to the elements obliterating all signs of life save the life of wind and rain. Examine the *stillness*, the *comfort*, the *trust* of the tramp in relation to *the weight of winter*. What is surprising in the word *comfort*? The tramp is not mentioned again. But what has he to do with *I ran* and with the carcasses on the keeper's gibbet? At the end what do poet and reader know?

We are all used to the excellent documentation of the wild that television offers. The wild enters the livingroom. The danger, of course, is a habit of passive viewing which reduces the technological triumph to a new form of domestication of the wild. Children whose imagination has been prompted into the activity demanded by a poem are more likely to bring activity to the film experience too, to go beyond the information given to reflection. A number of Ted Hughes's creature poems are wonderful matter for drawing young readers forward into new distances. My own favourite for classroom 'viewing' is *Pike*, a poem which gives the reader simultaneously the clarity and suspense of a first-class film and the activity of the observer's mind. Try borrowing from the film technique of visual image and voice-over to deepen participation in the first seven stanzas. For example, take the first stanza. Images: *pike, three inches long, green tigering the gold, grin, they dance on the surface among the flies*. Voice-over: *perfect pike in all parts, killers from the egg, malevolent, aged*. Then look at the fourth stanza. Images: close-up of *the jaw's hooked clamp and fangs, the gills kneading quietly, the pectorals*. Voice-over: *not to be changed at this date, a life subdued to its instrument*. Notice how little voice-over can be separated out in the fifth, sixth, seventh stanzas. But against that, how much of the last four stanzas can the camera reach? The pond, the lilies, the splashes, the owls, the woods—yes. But the monastery, the legendary depth, the pike, the fear, the *darkness beneath night's darkness*, the watching dream—what kind of seeing is this? What distance does imagination travel here?

Taking risks

The reader may notice in the preceding pages that poems are seldom indicated as suitable for a particular age or ability level. The pupils I have in mind are twelve- to fifteen-year-olds, but I found it quite impossible to be more specific than that. One thing the teacher learns by experience is not to underestimate the poetic reach of any audience. William Spouge describes the response to *Flying Crooked* (Graves) of a 'fifteen-year-old tough' who left school without taking an examination: 'He borrowed the book, copied down the poem laboriously and very neatly, and drew two lines through the script; one wayward and uncertain, the other a quite graceful flourish. He brought out his book and said: 'That's how it is, isn't it?' (**26**). One never knows for sure what is going to touch off that kind of independent collaboration. A non-academic thirteen-year-old whose attitude was often dismssive, greeted *The Wild Swans at Coole* (Yeats) with approval: 'Oh well, that's sensible'. Art can cause understanding where instruction can't. When imagination is awakened, it is impossible to predict limits of under-standing. Taking a risk with a 'difficult' poem may be the very thing that works when playing safe fails. There is an enormous psychological advantage in a risk that comes off, and little lost when it doesn't. Given the diversity of any class, it is rare for a risk to fail with all members.

One kind of poetry where it is worth taking risks is that suggested in chapter 2 in the section *The picture of nobody*. In this poetry the portable drama has a single character, the poet himself: loving, hating, rejoicing, suffering, believing, doubting. A way of handling a challenging poem of this kind is to change the usual order of reader/poem interaction, where the readers try to understand the poet, and to try instead how far the poet can go in understanding the reader. For example, take *Of Poor B.B.* (Brecht). How far into the readers' world and thinking will Brecht come? Can he recognize them, listen to them? To turn the tables like this can surprise pupils into thinking about questions they have not asked themselves before. It is a rewarding way, for instance, of handling poems which explore religious experience. Generally, the work of Skelton, Vaughan, Donne, Emily Dickinson can catch the ear and sensibility of fifteen-year-olds. Asking the poet what he has to say to them in their particular existence involves close attention to the signals available in the poem and leads to a firmer grasp of meaning.

Grouping poems which are related in content, but are of different complexity is a common way of clearing the path from the easily accessible to the more difficult. For example, *The Diviner* (Heaney) and *A Civil Servant* (Graves); poems by Clare and *Hawk Roosting* (Hughes). An adventurous kind of grouping which can have lively consequences is sometimes to make completely random choices. A member of the class simply opens the book at random. If the anthology has an arbitrary arrangement like the alphabetical arrangement of *The Rattle Bag*, the book is opened at one place. If the arrangement is thematic or chronological, the book is opened at two places, and one poem is chosen from each opening. The interest is in discovering whether the poems thrown together by the draw talk to one another. The situation has the merit of teacher as well as pupils starting from scratch.

Sometimes chance will reveal two poems deep in conversation. There is one beautiful coincidence in *The Rattle Bag*: *Perfect* (Hugh MacDiarmid) and *Pheasant* (Sylvia Plath) are on opposite pages. Knowing what is going on in *Pheasant* sets readers dead on course for sharing the leap of thought that occurs at the end of *Perfect*. More often, points of contact are less obvious, and there may not always be contact. It is usually necessary, particularly with bright pupils, to forestall over-ingenuity by making it clear that poems may refuse to have anything to do with one another.

A brief sample of what happens with second year pupils. A random opening of *Voices 2* gives *Death of a Naturalist* (Heaney) and *Reuben Bright* (E.A. Robinson). The two situations are identified: a child collecting tadpoles and a butcher whose wife has died. Some surface links are tried, such as the child's interest in the mess of frogspawn and the butcher's bloody work; some unproductive efforts made to match up the feeling of the child and the feeling of the butcher. The teacher suggested thinking in terms of two scraps of biography. 'They both run away from something. The boy runs away from the frogs, *the great slime kings*, the man runs away from *the slaughter-house*.' 'But it's not the same. The boy is only imagining that the slime kings are there. It's real for the butcher. His wife is dead.' 'It's real for the boy too. He says *I know that if I dipped my hand*.' 'One thing that's the same is the sadness afterwards. Reuben Bright was happy being a butcher, now his shop is no use to him anymore. The boy liked collecting tadpoles, now he's afraid of them.' 'I think they're both about being afraid. It's not the same fear, but it's just as real for the boy as for the butcher.' 'Changing. How you change when something changes your life.' 'Yes, the boy stops being a child and not minding how nasty the pond is. The man stops—well, he stops.'

The strategy is useful for all levels of ability, though the perception of relationships naturally varies greatly. It is useful also for small group work. What is particularly interesting and instructive for the teacher is the surprises he gets in the relationships pupils recognize without prompting.

Exploring meaning at different levels

Tact is of special importance when what lies between us and the class is a 'great' poem with the richness to reach home to readers of widely different experience and maturity. The challenge is to find the way through which the reaching home can happen for the particular audience, so that the peom is a possession that will grow in the possessing. What matters most, perhaps, in finding a way is respect for the pleasure of the audience at whatever level it appears to be occurring.

For example, Keats's *To Autumn*. The poem can be offered at any age, and can be returned to as the pupils grow, each time with a new understanding and a new perception of its life.

First and second year pupils
Entry for young readers is simply entry into the rich world immediately accessible in the surface layer, enjoyment of the sensation, of the feel of the thing. Collaborative activity is finding associations stirred in the imagination, taking in the pattern of sound through listening and saying, tasting in the mouth words familiar and unfamiliar. If the class has a fair experience of poetry, collaboration might involve discussion of how the sensations experienced by the reader are caused by the words the poet uses. Such exploration would not push the explorers further than selection of those words and phrases which they think are doing the work. Again, they would not be pressed to look for explanation of difficulties they choose to ignore. For instance, young readers seldom show signs of recognizing a problem in the second line, *close bosom-friend of the maturing sun.* They are usually too busy with their own ideas about autumn.

Third to fifth year pupils
Whether they have met the poem before or are meeting it for the first time, the starting-point is again the sensory impact of the upper surface. Then attention is turned towards observation of how the event is shaped. The growth of the poem is examined stanza by stanza. The

observers are asked to identify what senses the first stanza sets working. This is leading towards discovery that all the senses are assailed at once. Can seeing and touching, tasting, smelling, hearing be separated? How is the overlapping activity signalled in the words? What happens in the second stanza? What senses are set working here? Any change in how they are stirred? What change of focus causes this? How is the reader's experience affected by the four separate close-ups as against the mixed experience of the first stanza? Any change in pace? What has the 'human' activity to do with this? How does all this affect the reader's hold on the over-brimming richness of the first stanza? Set

> For Summer has o'er brimmed their clammy cells

against

> Thou watchest the last oozings hours by hours.

Then the third stanza. What now? What further change? This is the first time colour is named in the poem, and yet.... What is the landscape like now? Which sense takes over and dominates as the stanza moves forward? What has happened to the sound-value of the language? What has happened between the first line of the poem and the last?

What the exploration is leading towards is recognition that the poem in every particular acts out the steady shift of the earth from autumn to winter. Whether one tempts the class further than that understanding depends on one's judgement of their stamina and maturity. With many groups, to try explicitly for a deeper entry may be unwise. But where response to the exploration so far shows ease, it is worth moving towards the way the poem enacts the relationship between time and change, the perception of time as the source of all movement. A way to approach this is to set the pupils thinking about the two questions in the poem:

> Who hath not seen thee oft amid thy store?

and

> Where are the songs of Spring? Ay, where are they?

What associations does the word *store* evoke? But what about the second question? How is the first question itself questioned in the second, and set aside? Is the recognition of the store slipping out of grasp a new seeing or something the poem knows from the beginning? Look back at the first stanza. How many words there signal change? Follow the current of time/change words running right through the poem. This is the moment the kind of change underlying the third stanza lights up for the readers, as they follow the current there: *soft-dying,   wailful,   mourn,   sinking,   lives   or   dies,   now . . .*

They seldom fail to come upon the calm interplay of beginnings and endings.

Sixth form pupils
At this stage ordinarily the poem appears in the context of other Keats poems. The natural and fruitful approach is to study *To Autumn* in relation to the great May odes, in the hope of leading towards some understanding of the advance in wisdom between May and September of 'the marvellous year'; towards recognizing *To Autumn* as the final identification of what is sought so passionately in the odes. After study of the May poems, certain knowledge of the letters of the intervening summer prepares for study of *To Autumn* (**13**). The summer letters are marked by weariness and unease; those to Fanny Brawne show an increasing restlessness in the relationship, jealousies and perturbations. But the letters written in September during a stay at Winchester suggest a mastered calm, a calm he wants to hold on to. Back in London for a few days, he writes to Fanny Brawne to explain why he will not visit her: 'As far as they regard myself, I can despise all events: but I cannot cease to love you. . . . I am a Coward. I cannot bear the pain of being happy: it is out of the question: I must admit no thought of it.' (Letter 191). A week later, back in Winchester, he writes to Reynolds, and speaks of his pleasure in the lovely autumn weather: 'really, without joking, chaste weather—Dian skies—I never liked stubble fields so much as now—Aye better than the chilly green of the spring. Somehow a stubble field looks warm—in the same way that some pictures look warm—this struck me so much in my Sunday's walk that I composed upon it.' (Letter 193). On the same day he begins a letter to Woodhouse and completes it the following day. This is the letter which contains the first version of *To Autumn* (Letter 194).

The poem would first be explored in itself. This is essential if the pupils have not met the poem before, or have not studied it in any detail. Then it is set beside the odes. A starting point is the correspondence of the external conditions of composition: the fine weather of the three weeks during which the May poems were written, the lovely autumn which Keats described to Reynolds. (In another September letter, he writes of the effect on men of their physical environment.) Now to the deeper correspondence. Recall the students' understanding of the reflection on the nature of vision in the May odes: experience of vision, intense effort to know and hold the experience, recognition of inevitable fading of vision. In what sense is *To Autumn* an enactment of the fading of vision? Significance of *keep steady thy laden head* against the *sometimes . . . sometimes* of the second stanza? Recall the shape of reflection in the odes—particularly how each ends in regret, and the need to 'understand' the inevitable fading: the *vanishing phantoms* of *On Indolence*; the *cloudy trophies hung* of *On Melancholy*; the question at the end of *To a Nightingale*; the statement at the end of *On a Grecian Urn*, but in *To Autumn* the absence of any such need. Consider the poem as itself enactment of the fading as a beautiful thing. Watch what happens to the figure of Autumn as the poem grows. And at the end? Compare the presence of the poet in this poem with his presence in the odes. Consider the poem as complete achievement of 'negative capability without any irritable reaching after fact and reason'(**13**).

4

'Minutely appropriate words'

(William Blake)

In the methods of presentation so far suggested, the main emphasis has been on what a poem is communicating, what imaginative activity it sets going in the reader. The conscious focus of attention has been on what the poem achieves, not on how it does so. It is the *how*, the craft of poetry, that concerns us in this chapter. What can we do to help young readers to share in the pleasure of knowing something of how the artefact works?

Investigating the craft of the poet has little point if it does not lead to an increase of pleasure and satisfaction. Knowledge of craft is a natural part of a developed response to something that pleases us. Being able to recognize how this works satisfies our fascination with pattern and increases our ability to take it into stock. We like watching in slow motion a flower opening or a footballer scoring a goal, because slow motion reveals the beautiful complex harmony of movement. In the matter of poetry there is the value of a greater awareness of what can be done with the common gift of language, of seeing that it can enact feeling as well as refer to it. 'Language which is able to power a lift is most often used to operate a doorbell'(**27**). Some knowledge of how poets make language power a lift is a counterbalance to the daily use of it to operate doorbells. Most importantly, knowing something of how poetry works means knowing more about one's own human equipment. This matters greatly in our approach to the study of craft: it should reinforce the young reader's sense of *his* essential contribution, *his* power to receive communications.

'Enjamblement'

Why a poem should work as it does is an exceedingly complex question still in the asking. Only a fraction of the number of elements that come together in the making of a poem is matter for investigation in the classroom. At any level the amount that can be dealt with is naturally limited. This makes it all the more important that what is done should not be reductive in effect, but should develop a sense of the richness of the way poetic language behaves.

A common risk in dealing with the question of craft is the 'enjamblement' effect. Enjamblement is the practice of searching a poem for the number of rhetorical devices it contains. I owe the term to this comment:

'The *long vowels and assonance* help the rhythm and the flow of words bring out the idea of the moon rising in the East. The commas are used in very suitable places. The enjamblement quickens up the pace. The *Caesura*.'

The writer was then appropriately stuck. My prize example of the enjamblement effect is the following:

'The language is simple: the words are impeccably chosen there is inevitability of epithets, the adjectives are few yet wielded with deadly accuracy. The Redskin's speech is elliptical.'

The subject of these unhappily earnest comments is a story in a comic from which the exhortation 'Go it, Pa, singe the pants off the kidnappin' varmint' is a fair sample of its verbal elegance.

Examples may not always be so arresting, but the habit of trotting out the names of rhetorical figures instead of observing the language in a particular poem is a phenomenon familiar to examiners. It is the consequence of the glossary approach, starting with definitions of technical terms and examples out of context. When we begin investigating how the language of poetry works, it is important not to confuse the issue by providing pupils with a set of labels. The labels get between the young reader and the poem, and imply that a new vocabulary has to be learned before one can say what one notices. Besides, they involve us in definitions so reductive as to be inaccurate. There is, for example, that definition of a metaphor still with us: 'a comparison without the use of *like* or *as*'.

The glossary approach reduces the question of craft to a game called Spot-the-Figures-of-Speech or at a later level Hunt-the-Symbol. Terms should never be given before discovery of the language act they name at work in a poem. Pupils can describe what they notice without benefit of such terms. 'The word *mashed* is an ordinary word used in an extraordinary way. It makes you know how the storm is pushing everything around and down like when you mash potatoes with a potatomasher.' (Second year pupil: *An awful tempest mashed the air* Emily Dickinson). 'The way he says *cl* at the beginning of two words makes it seem that he is so happy that he is stuttering.' (Third year pupil: *Spring* Hopkins) The trouble about starting with terms is that they fail to make clear what those comments make clear; that the parts of the pattern work their effect only in the context of the whole. Pupils who are trying to get the terms right tend to stop when they have identified the figure instead of going on to think about what happens because of the metaphor or alliteration. What we want to teach is the fact that the effect of any figure depends on the pattern in which it occurs. For example, the alliteration in '*Before it cloud, before it cloy*' (*Spring* Hopkins) has not the same effect as that in '*He clasps the crag with crooked hands*' (*The Eagle* Tennyson).

To prevent the enjamblement effect, there are some basic principles worth keeping in mind. Investigation of craft should not become an end in itself. It is valuable only in so far as it deepens enjoyment and understanding. Thus, the decision to study the craft of any poem depends upon the poem. Always one weighs the possible gain against the kind of effort the exercise demands. The aspects of craft brought to attention should be confined to those which will enable inexperienced readers to see the relationship between craft and meaning. Investigation should always start from inside a given poem, not from outside, not with isolated snippets of verse which exemplify this or that stylistic device. Technical terms should be used sparingly, introduced gradually, and not used at all if their use is likely to shake confidence and cause anxiety. Pacing is important; we need to think of skill in observation as developing over a number of years, not weeks.

The suggestions made in this chapter vary in level of difficulty. They have all been tried in the classroom, but not all with every class I have worked with. The majority represent work done with third, fourth and fifth year pupils of average to high ability. There are situations where the teacher will rightly decide that the question of craft will seldom become any more explicit than it is in the approaches described in previous chapters. How a poem is achieving its effect will be a matter for attention only when there is a clear signal from the class that the question is worth raising. It was a semi-literate indifferent fifth year pupil who had this to say about *The Windhover* (Hopkins): 'It's the word *caught* that gets you—it catches you like—it catches you like he catches the bird—sort of sudden like—he caught the bird and the poem catches you—so you sort of catch the bird too like he does—in the poem.' The effort opened the eyes and ears of other members of the class who began to be interested in how they had been 'caught'.

'It makes you know'

'The work of verbal art . . . has a structure which is neither objective nor subjective, but *intersubjective*. The reader who wishes to discuss with others his reaction to a work relies on the fact that his reactions and theirs *share* certain features . . . If I miss something, you can "*show*" me that it is there'(**28**) (My italics.)

Examining the craft of poetry is a matter of showing. It is not only the teacher who shows. The starting-point is the showing that is done by the pupils themselves. It is unwise, I think, to plan a systematic introduction of the different elements of poetic craft. The principle of working from inside a poem means that there is no particular order to be followed. It is better to follow the direction which the children's response suggests, to trust their natural capacity to take part in the intersubjective dialogue. The pupil who commented on the word *mashed* is doing exactly what we want to happen, showing the link between pattern and reader. So was a pupil who said about the lines,

> The waves beside them danced; but they
> Outdid the sparkling waves in glee.

> *The Daffodils*   (Wordsworth)

'You can imagine the daffodils are living things and have a mind of their own so that they can be happy or sad when they like. You get a joyful feeling about the daffodils because they seem to be having a wonderful time and they show it by being giddy and lightheaded. They give happiness and brightfulness to everyone.'

That would not be an occasion for telling the speaker she needs the term *personification*. She patently does not need it. A pupil clutching the term would be unlikely to find the inspired phrase, 'giddy and light-headed'. The term belongs to a later stage after several such recognitions have occurred.

The answer to the question of what to do about the craft of a poem with first and second year pupils is: wait and see what the children do. During a practice lesson a student teacher was reading *The Lesson* (Edward Lucie-Smith) with a mixed ability first year class. Having listened to the poem, one pupil said, 'I don't see why he's talking about goldfish. Another said, 'Well, they were there—on the shelf. He saw them.' The talk moved away then to the event: the boy's way of taking the news of his father's death, the puzzle of his relief, of *grief has its uses*, his unhappiness at school, the odd effects of shock and so on. Then with the boy's feeling of pride at the end of the poem, the goldfish were back and the original objector again demanded an explanation of their presence. The supervisor suggested gathering together the variety of feelings in the poem. The children listed shock, relief, fear, shame, self-consciousness, pride. Then one of them said, 'Oh I *see*—it's all the different feelings swimming around inside you (rubbing her midriff) like goldfish in a bowl and different ones come up.'

Again, what is valuable in that example is the recognition that something which appeared odd at first sight 'makes you know'. 'Ideas', said Blake, 'cannot be given except in their minutely appropriate words.' If we can get young readers to trust their intuitive understanding of this fact and give them plenty of opportunity to show what *they* notice, they are well-equipped to enjoy what *we* have to show. The emphasis of our showing is always on making bright the contact between poem and reader.

Some explorations: first and second year

'If no surprise for the reader, none for the writer, and vice versa' (**10**). In the early stages it is naturally the obvious surprise that readers are caught by. The alertness they show spontaneously is a first step towards the more subtle surprises they will recognize later. The 'goldfish' example is an instance of what pupils in the lower school notice unprompted.

Dissection (Colin Rowbotham)
This is an accessible model of how a poet may go behind the scenes of an ordinary event and persuade the reader to follow by surprising him. What are *marzipan*, *crucify*, *torn by the eye*, *a small machine* doing in a poem about dissecting a rat? It is an odd mixture. How does it work on the reader—if it does work?

Blackberry-Picking (Seamus Heaney)
This is a good piece for accustoming children to the fact that a poetic image is not necessarily visual. Since the word *image* is familiar, it can be used from the start without need for explanation. Borrow the analogy of a map at an underground station where you press a button and a chain of lights picks out your journey. Start with *a glossy purple clot* and see how the image persuades the reader to bring his own experience into action. Then follow the chain of lights/images through the poem and test their helpfulness for the readers. What lights set them thinking of unexpected connections? Will they pass a *plate of eyes*? Look back over the chain. How many of the lights are pointing them towards the disappointment at the end of the poem? Does the chain help a reader who has never gone blackberrying to know what it is like?

Nile Fishermen (Rex Warner)
The context of *Blackberry-Picking* is familiar northern summer whether the actual event is familiar or not. *Nile Fishermen* comes out of another continent. Explore the three-part relationship: the fishermen, the watching poet, the reader. The first and third meet in the words of the second. Again a chain of images marks out the route of the meeting. Sight images: fishermen, ropes, river. Words that make the reader see? The context of sun and water in the third stanza. What is happening in *sun is torn in coloured petals*, *crescents*, *clipping wings*, *seagull sails*? Sensation images: the movement of the fishermen at work. Words that make the reader feel their action physically? Sight and sensation images running into one another. Why *swimming* round, a joke *stirs*? Sound images: when do they start? Suggest a word to describe the effect of the scene on the poet. How does the chain of images draw the reader into sharing the poet's judgement, not the police officials'? Think about the vividness of the strong bodies. What about the *officials* who are also

part of what the poet saw? Take the last two lines as the destination of meaning arrived at. The lights go out and the reader is left to decide the meaning for himself. What does he decide?

The Eagle (Tennyson)
Start not with Tennyson's eagle, but with the children's. What would they expect to find in a poem about the bird? Collect and record suggestions: keen sight, fierceness, speed, strength, nesting habits, beak, how an eagle attacks its prey. Read the poem. Do any of the words recorded on the board occur in the poem? Yet it is all there. Match up the two versions. What sensation enters with the poem that wasn't there in the first stage? Why bring the sea into it as well as the sky? Can anyone speak for the words *wrinkled* and *crawled*? Try un-rhyming the poem, replacing end-rhymes by other words. For example, *hands—claws, stands—waits, walls—perch, falls—dives*. *Claws* would continue the run of 'k' sounds in *clasps, crags, crooked, close*. But is *hands* doing something else besides rhyming with *stands*? Test what is lost in the other substitutions besides rhyme. If the children are linguistically advanced, let them loose on *like a thunderbolt*. Is it worth its place? Judgements vary on the matter.

Stopping by Woods on a Snowy Evening (Robert Frost)
This poem has no obvious surprise, no dazzle of ingenuity. The surprise is much deeper and young readers are rarely conscious of being surprised. That they are shows in their readiness to linger with the poem. When they have explored the event and speculated about the ending, take them on to the way the poem enacts falling snow. Evoke their knowledge of watching snow fall, the hypnotic effect it has. Tell them, if no one comes up with the fact, that if you stare upwards long enough into falling snow it looks black, not white. How does the poem make you know all this? Inevitably, young readers make for the lines,

> The only other sound's the sweep
> Of easy wind and downy flake.

Examine the pattern of matching sounds there. If you repeat the lines often enough they have the same drowsy effect as falling snow. Those matching sounds—does that happen only in these lines? The first response to this question is usually to point to the end-rhymes. Look at the pattern of rhyme, the way rhymes are carried over from stanza to stanza. As one child put it: 'It's like the snow. There's no real break. The same rhymes at the end make it seem as if the snow won't ever stop falling.' But is it only the end of lines that match? In the two lines quoted the sounds are matched inside the lines. Does that happen anywhere else? Observation reveals that echo begins in the first line and works right through: words beginning with the same letter, words

with the same vowel sound, whole words repeated, a whole line repeated. All this is happening so naturally that you don't notice it till
you look closely, filling up in the reader's mind like the snow filling up
the woods. Does this help with the *promises* question? How does the
patterning let the reader into the poet's mind, into the way he is
tempted by watching woods fill up with snow? How children respond to
this question varies. Sometimes the whole event appears to remain
literal for them and in that case they should not, I think, be pressed
further. But sometimes there is a flash of perception that

> The woods are lovely, dark and deep

is not as straightforward as it seems.

Humming-Bird (Lawrence). *A route of evanescence* (Emily Dickinson)
Two ways of recording the extraordinariness of the humming-bird,
both difficult, but worth trying with alert first and second year groups.
Humming-Bird makes a direct challenge to the reader to keep up with
Lawrence's 'whizzing' imagination: *I can imagine, I believe, Probably, We
look at him through the wrong end of the telescope of time*. The words invite the
reader to participate in speculation. The poem needs to be read slowly,
following the deliberate pace of the phrasing. It helps to pick up the
analogy of the telescope and give time to focus properly on each
magnified image. Most of the poem looks through the right end and
finds a huge *other world*. What words persuade the reader to bring his
own sense of the primeval world into play? Where does the telescope
swing over so that for a moment we are looking through the wrong end?
Why should the minute bird launch the poet on such a flight through
distance?
A route of evanescence should be taken fast. The interest is in the way the
language enacts the bird's speed and colour. Read the poem after
Lawrence's without telling the class the subject. Emily Dickinson gives
no title. Let it be a riddle. Occasionally someone recognizes the subject
straightaway; more often the riddle is solved by exploring what is
happening in the language. Once the colour and breathless speed are
recognized, the clues of the images fall into place. Have the two poems
anything in common apart from the subject?

A Gentle Echo (Swift)
Instead of reading the poem whole, uncover it bit by bit. Read the first
eight lines. What is the poet up to in the question/answer arrangement?
What tricks does he play to make a rhyme? For the rest of the piece,
give the question without the answer. Invite suggestions before un-
covering Swift's solution, reminding the collaborators of possible
options noticed in the first eight lines and of the necessity to give a
sensible answer to the Shepherd's question. Most of the solutions will be

the same as Swift's. *Her dear* is likely to stump them, and Swift's solution to fall flat. So is the *wind/wind* rhyme, unless someone remembers that *wind* meaning the element used to rhyme with *kind* in older poetry. The point of the exercise is that the slowing down shows up how the piece works; by arousing the reader's curiosity about how the poet will solve the problem he sets himself. Whether attention is drawn to the play with the word *gentle* in title and poem depends on the linguistic sophistication of the class.

The investigation might be linked with rhyme-play in humorous verse (limericks, clerihews, epigrams) where rhyme is clearly a weapon not for show but for use.

Autobiography (Louis MacNeice). *The Gallows* (Edward Thomas)

Refrain is a feature of patterning which children notice themselves and how it works in the poem/reader contact is a question which can be raised with pupils in the lower school. In *The Bailey beareth the bell away* (see chapter 3) individual interpretation of the event is influenced by whether the refrain is heard as a signal of happiness or as a signal of sadness. The refrain in *Autobiography* has the challenge of a riddle. Why add a riddle to the poem? The story itself is quite clear—or is it? What *did* happen? An actual loss of a parent or a childish fear uncomforted? The speaker was five when the event took place. How sure can we be of the accuracy of an early memory? Does the refrain help in how the reader understands what happened? Remember what it was like going to bed as a child, the last 'goodnight', the light going out . . . *Come back early or never come* . . . Has the refrain a different effect by the end of the poem?

Refrain in *The Bailey beareth the bell away* and in *Autobiography* invites the reader to take physical part in the poem, as many ballads do. In *The Gallows* the interesting thing is the way the reader is both tempted to join in and held back from joining in. Thomas gives the impression of using refrain without in fact doing so, apart from the repetition of *On the dead oak tree bough*. Set the class to observe how the 'refrain' parts of the stanzas are linked, with straight repetitions, shifting repetitions, changes in the expected pattern. The 'refrain' lines create a sad feeling. They also make the reader *see*, as he listens to the swinging sound, what started off the poet on making the poem; the sight of dead creatures swinging from a branch. Now look at how the refrain part of a stanza is attached to the other part, how the colours of the two parts of the pattern run into one another. So the reader is drawn into thinking with the poet as well as watching with him.

A word at work

'The chief difference between the language in poems and the language outside poems is that the one is more highly structured than the other,

and the more complex organization set up in poems makes it possible
for the poet to redress and exploit various characteristics of language at
large' (**8**). Any language-user can come up with fresh images or ingenious rhymes. The gift of the poet is that he orders these in a pattern in
which the parts answer one another, are interdependent. 'The poem is
not a collection of phrases, but a dramatic action, the actors being such
things as metres, alterations of tone and so on' (**8**). It is a keen alertness
to this 'dramatic action' that we want to foster as the pupils' experience
of poetic language increases. It is essential to keep the emphasis always
on the relation of the part to the whole. In order to show this we have to
isolate elements, but it needs always to be clear that the elements
isolated draw their power from the behaviour of the other actors in the
drama.

It is wise to seize every opportunity for reinforcing the notion that
words in a poem work together, even where we do not intend to
examine the craft of a given poem in detail. It is worth, for instance,
making precise examination of the working of a single word or phrase a
fairly regular practice, whatever the main emphasis of attention. Before
discussion of a poem closes, someone is invited to select an item for
investigation. The selected item is then investigated by the whole
group.

A narrow fellow in the grass (Emily Dickinson). The words *Whip lash*
Collect the associations called up by the words in isolation: speed,
suppleness, alarm, sting. Look at the words working with the immediate
neighbours: *unbraiding, wrinkled, was gone*. What implications of the word
are picked up and made precise there? Go back to *barefoot*: why give
that one detail about the boy? Then investigate how *Whip lash* strikes off
other words elsewhere in the poem—*narrow, sudden, a tighter breathing,
zero at the bone*.

Welsh Incident (Graves). The words *I was coming to that*
Selection may fasten on the indefinable, as happened when a pupil
chose the repetition of *I was coming to that*. Investigation threw up a
number of suggestions: the impossibility throughout of describing the
marvellous things that came out from the sea-caves, the persistence of
the questions (like children listening to a story), the efforts of the story-
teller to do the impossible (he can describe the reception but not the
things). The real triumph was that someone said that choosing that line
was doing the same thing as the questioners in the poem; asking a
question that could not be answered.

The Sentry (Wilfred Owen) The words *deluging muck*
The interest here is in the meaning of *deluging*, which gathers up the
ceaseless onslaught, and the sound-value of *muck*. Observation reveals

that the broad 'u' and 'k' of the word dominate the poem up to the finding of the sentry's body, when the sounds thin out. Further thought should lead to the unspoken word *destruction*.

Woefully Arrayed (Skelton). The words *woefully arrayed*
Examine the sound-relation of the repeated *woefully arrayed* to the whole poem, in particular the 'ay' sound and the emphatic final 'd'. Connection with the impression of suffering? Connection between the modification of the sound in the last two stanzas and the change in tone there?

The Darkling Thrush (Hardy). The word *haunted*
First the logical meaning. The people who frequent the place (compare 'he haunts the place'), presumably those who live in the district. *Haunted* is a curious choice in the context. On the one hand, it picks up *spectre-grey*; on the other, it clashes with the emptiness of the landscape. It draws attention to itself by its oddity. Try another possibility for the line: 'And all the folk who lived nearby'. *Folk* is a Hardy word, but he chose the less straightforward *all mankind that haunted nigh*. A contradiction? Allow that he wants the word *haunted* because other associations of the word match the atmosphere and mood so well. But why does he want *all mankind*? Move out from the line to the rest of the poem. Where else does the grief gather in the whole world?

In Time of Pestilence (Nashe). The line *I am sick, I must die*
First, the emotional impact of the two-stroke recurrence, the link with the tolling bell and with the other recurring line *Lord, have mercy on us*. Associations the reader makes? Then the difference between this line and the rest of the poem. Here the first person, *I*. Elsewhere? Next the two-part shape of the line and the shape of several other lines throughout the poem. How often does a line or a pair of lines strike contrasting notes: death against life, sickness against health, weakness against strength, ugliness against beauty? If the class can mark stress, try setting the rhythm of *I am sick, I must die* against the rhythmic pattern of the poem as a whole. The point is that in the rest of the poem the frequent strong stressing of the first word in each line enacts the slight gasp that comes between the strokes of a bell. The reader finds himself echoing this in the reading. The effect is heard most readily in the several lines where the second syllable also is stressed. For example:

> Death proves them all but toys . . .
> Gold cannot buy you wealth . . .
> Strength stoops unto the grave . . .

On his Blindness (Milton). The word *lodg'd*
Examine the possible meanings of the word *lodge*: living in another

house temporarily, deposited with, driven in like a weapon, hard to remove, crops flattened by rain. Examine *lodg'd* in its immediate context of the parable of the Talents. Logically, it has the meaning 'deposited with'. Emotionally, how many of the other meanings are at work? Relation between the passive *lodg'd useless* and the words *stand and wait* in the last line?

Rhythm and metre

Watching words at work in a particular context develops the pupils' ability to recognize the figures of sense and figures of sound that poets use. Experience of obvious figures over a number of poems reinforces grasp of the fact that poetic pattern is not simply pattern-making for its own sake, but an instrument of meaning. Eventually, some terms can be given for convenience of reference, when the teacher is sure that the new words correspond to knowledge already possessed. The language gesture that fuses knowledge from different areas can be identified as metaphor; the gesture that puts two different pieces of knowledge side by side can be identified as simile. Further refinements such as metonymy and synecdoche are unnecessary. Figures of sound can be given their names. Rhyme the pupils know already. For other ways of matching sounds that have been noticed, the terms alliteration and assonance can be given.

The question of rhythm and metre is more complicated. That verse has rhythm is something the ear knows from early childhood, and plenty of listening to verse refines and extends the satisfaction this gives. Generally, pupils are quite capable of describing obvious rhythmic trends: slow, hurrying, smooth, jogging, cheerful, sad, thoughtful, and so on. How the effect is achieved—the relationship between rhythm and metre—is a much more difficult question, and little can be done in this area until sixth form work. Younger pupils can, and I think should, learn how to mark stress, but the complex business of identifying different metric patterns is rarely worth the labour involved. Even pupils who succeed in mastering the four basic metres (iambus, trochee, anapaest, dactyl) are unable to do anything with the knowledge beyond mechanical identification. Besides, the knowledge is not a reliable tool. The real interest of English metrics is the range of variation poets actually use. There are always at least two patterns running against one another: the conventional verse metre and the metre of natural speech. For example,

> The quality of mercy is not strained

can be scanned as regular iambic pentameter, but no user of English will speak it like that. The relation between the verse metre of the line and what a speaker can do with it is a fascinating question too complex for everyday classroom discussion.

Energy should, I suggest, be given to developing the children's natural capacity to respond to rhythm, to identify the effect it has on the reader, and to discover the relationship between rhythm and meaning. Understanding of the rhythm/meaning connection is most easily strengthened when there is a rhythmic surprise, an unexpected turn in the pattern.

In *The Ballad of Rudolph Reed* (Gwendolyn Brooks) there is a sudden disruption of rhythm and rhyme in the stanza:

> For were they not firm in a home of their own
> With windows everywhere
> And a beautiful banistered stair
> And a front yard for flowers and a back yard for grass?

Listeners notice the jolt without prompting. Why should it happen just there? What change of feeling does it match? How does the story begin for a moment to be a different story at that point?

Death, be not proud (Donne) contains an easily understood rhythmic surprise in the line

> One short sleep past, we wake eternally

What happens to the flow of rhythm at the beginning of the line? Why should the river of sound meet a rock at that point? Connect the surprise of rhythm with the surprise of thought that follows in the next line: *Death, thou shalt die.*

For older pupils both *The Going* and *The Voice* (Hardy) show a rhythmic awkwardness serving communication. The last stanza of *The Going* begins,

> Well, well! All's past amend
> Unchangeable. It must go.

It is impossible to force rhythmic smoothness on the lines, particularly on *It must go*. How does the stumble enact the receding of remembrance and Hardy's bleak recognition of the irreversible?

The last stanza of *The Voice* sets off on a different rhythmic shape from the rest of the poem. Again, how does the change enact meaning?

See also in this chapter the comments on *In Time of Pestilence* (Nashe) and *Because I Could Not Stop for Death* (Emily Dickinson), and in chapter 3, the comments on *Snake* (Lawrence) and *The Red Wheelbarrow* (William Carlos Williams).

Whether to deal with metre as well as rhythm is a matter of choice. In my experience, pupils of average ability and interest enjoy the business of discovering stress-pattern. If metre is to be dealt with, the important thing again is that it should be introduced in a context where the function of metre is very clear.

Humorous verse with a clear stress-pattern is lively material for showing how to discover patterns. *Death of a Mad Dog* (Goldsmith) is a useful example. Set the class to beat out the rhythm emphatically and show them how to represent graphically what their ear tells them, using / for stress and ⌣ or ✕ for non-stress. If there is uncertainty about whether a syllable should be marked or not, add the sign \ for a doubtful stress. For example, the word *both* in the line,

<blockquote>Bòth móngrĕl, púppў, whélp aňd hóund</blockquote>

Notice the pattern ⌣ ⟋ that shows up in the graphic representation.

Try finding the stress pattern in part of a poem they enjoy saying. Take the last stanza of *Macavity: the Mystery Cat* (T. S. Eliot) for example. Hammer out the rhythm aloud; tumpety-tump rather than with normal emphasis. As the lines are being read, the graphic representation is appearing on the blackboard. A jolt comes with *Macavity wasn't there!* Replace the words with those used up to now, *Macavity's not there*. Now there's no jolt and the rest of the stanza works its way home steadily. The graphic representation shows a series of ⌣ ⟋ with some variations ⌣ ⌣ ⟋. Then try reading each line with normal emphasis, checking the result against the pattern discovered. What strong stresses now slip down to doubtful stresses? Is there still a definite pattern? There ought to be disagreement about lines 6 and 8. Now restore *Macavity wasn't there*. Efforts to force this into either pattern simply won't work. What is the poet up to? He could have used the words that do fit. Readers see quickly that the jolt in the pattern makes the most important thing about Macavity stand out dramatically.

The Listeners (de la Mare) gives an impression of rhythmic regularity, but observation of the metric pattern reveals why different readers can read it in different ways. Take odd lines for investigation and watch how a reader has a choice of where to place the stress. Generally, however, even when there is disagreement about some syllables, the stress is distributed fairly evenly over the line. The feature that fascinates young readers when they discover it is the unusual stress-pattern in those lines which convey what is going on *inside* the house. Use a natural speech stressing:

<blockquote>
Stóod lísteňiňg iň tħe qúiĕt ŏf tħe móonliğht . . .
Stóod thróngiňg tħe faínt móon beăms oň tħĕ dárk stáir . . .
Heárkeňiňg iň aň aír stiŕred aňd sháken . . .
Féll échŏiňg thróugh tħe shádŏwiňĕss ŏf tħe stíll hoúse . . .
</blockquote>

The strong stresses coming together force the reader to slow his pace. The clusters of non-stresses huddling between stresses, particularly striking in the last line quoted, enact the shadowy movement of the phantom listeners.

Shape and meaning

The relationship between form and meaning, the outer visible journey of
a poem enacting the inner journey of the poet's imagination, is implicit in
a number of explorations suggested in this chapter. The relationship can
be shown more explicitly in certain poems where the pupils can discover
for themselves how the shape a poet chooses is an important part of the
way he communicates with the reader.

For example, they have the equipment to identify the borrowing of the
chain convention from nursery rhymes in *The Responsibility* (Peter
Appleton). The Bomb and childhood—why bring the two together like
this? What has it to do with making the reader think and feel? Follow the
snowball effect. Watch the play with *I, he, they*. What understanding has
been gathered when the snowball stops rolling? Who in fact is the *I*
responsible?

The North Ship (Philip Larkin)

Another poem which borrows the shape of the nursery-rhyme, this 'legend'
is clearly deeper and darker than the nursery rhyme it starts from: *I saw three
ships come sailing by*. But the nursery rhyme link is relevant. The reader is
beckoned to follow as he once followed the bit by bit revelation of the old
rhyme with its comforting repetitions. How is the reader drawn into
realizing that *The North Ship* is not childhood play, drawn into taking the
poem seriously? At first all seems well. Notice the behaviour of sea and wind
in the first two stanzas. Sensations, associations, of *lifting, running*? In the
third stanza the uneasiness begins. There is a new suspense to sharpen
attention. Examine *quaking, hunted like a beast, anchor*. And then? How is the
north ship cut off from the others in the language used: *drove, darkening, no
breath of wind*? The word *sky* returns, this time with menace. What ending
does the reader begin to fear? What ending does he find? What sea is the
third ship travelling – without a wind? As to meanings: the outer journey
takes the ship *wide and far*; the inner journey takes the reader where? The
question is for individual reflection, each reader examining the thoughts the
poem provokes for him.

A Rope for Harry Fat (James Baxter)

This provides a similar opportunity. What connection is there between
the street-ballad form and the poet's desire to make his anger and pity
public, to make everyone listen? Investigate what he does with the form.
What is unusual about the title? Where does the poet use language that
belongs to another kind of writing? What has this to do with the message
received? Who is this Harry Fat?

To Daffodils (Herrick)

Use to show how the visible shape on the page as well as the audible
shape expresses the writer's thinking and feeling. 'You could blow it

away like a bubble' was how a thirteen-year-old described the effect of
the poem. Investigating how the effect is achieved reveals first the faint
echoes of sound throughout. Then turn to the line-arrangement. Listen
to the hovering effect of the first two lines, where the sense draws the
reader on but the line break holds him back for a second. Where else
does that happen? Connect this to the idea of daffodils fading and the
poet's regret. Look at the shape of the poem on the page. All the lines
are short, but four stand out as shorter still:

> Stay . . .
> Has run. . . .
> We die . . .
> Away . . .

Think of them as a sort of poem around which the rest of the poem
moves. How do these lines signal the centre of the poet's thinking and
feeling?

The Darkling Thrush (Hardy)

Once when a fourth year group were studying *The Darkling Thrush*, a
pupil asked why Hardy had not set it out in four-line stanzas, since
there was no rhyme-link across the eight lines of each stanza. The
question started up an investigation which yielded the following discovery. The first stanza sets up an actual physical scene: a man leans
on a gate, noticing the signs of winter in a frozen landscape. In the
second stanza the watcher interprets the scene, linking it with his own
hopelessness. In the third stanza his meditation is interrupted by the
thrush. As in the first stanza it is an actual physical event which holds
his attention. The fourth stanza, like the second, is an attempt to
interpret what is actually there. So the stanza arrangement makes
sense. The journey of Hardy's thought was the clearer for the investigation.

The Collar (Herbert)

It was a fifth year pupil who drew attention to an interesting feature of
the rhyming in *The Collar*. The class had examined the wavering
rhymes, the unpredictability of when a rhyme would occur, and had
linked this to Herbert's spiritual distress. Then one of them pointed to
the special case of the *me—thee—see* rhyme, saying that it took Herbert
nine lines to reach a rhyme for *me* (a longer gap than occurs with any
other rhyme) and then quickly he finds the third rhyme *see*. Her point
was that the gap between *me* and *thee* reflected Herbert's struggle to
submit and the quicker return of the rhyme reflected his beginning to
do so. Someone else suggested that the quicker return matched the
'tightening' of the collar, which prompted yet another to draw attention
to the fact that after *see* a rhyme from the very beginning of the poem

returns again, in *abroad*. An interesting example of how pupils can do the showing.

The sonnet form

The ease with which pupils can be taught to mark the rhyme-scheme of a sonnet tempts us to start with the outer convention of the form. This seems to me a mistaken approach. It reduces a poem to a rhyme-scheme and gets in the way of discovering the real beauty of the form: the correspondence of outer and inner form in a true sonnet. Further, the fourteen-lines-fixed-rhyme-scheme notion causes problems of appreciating experiments with the form. Hopkins' 'curtal' sonnet, for instance, where the proportion 8:6 becomes 6:4½. *Pied Beauty* is an example the pupils are likely to meet in an anthology. Another variation is the use of the outer form of the English sonnet with the inner form of the Italian sonnet. Shakespeare's *Shall I Compare Thee to a Summer's Day* and Wilfred Owen's *Anthem for the Doomed Youth* are examples.

We should, I think, start with the poem, not with the rhyme-scheme, encourage discovery of the two-part structure of thought, and draw attention to the outer shape only when the pupils have met a number of sonnets without hearing the term *sonnet*. The special fascination of the form is then more likely to cause satisfaction. 'He explains in the second part what he sees in the first' (*Pied Beauty* Hopkins). 'The first part is the feeling of Spring itself. The second part is what Spring makes him think' (*Spring* Hopkins). 'At first it's the thrill of his own discovery of a book. It's like a journey to new places. Then it is other discoveries, discovering a new planet or a new continent' (*Chapman's Homer* Keats). 'Owen moves from the terrible noise of the battle to the quiet sadness of those who will always remember the dead soldiers' (*Anthem for the Doomed Youth* Wilfred Owen). This kind of discovery is what matters first. Then seeing that the rhyme-scheme has a matching shape has itself the quality of discovery.

Ways of saying

The term *diction* is better avoided till sixth form work, but what it stands for is not beyond the grasp of younger pupils, provided that the matter is raised only where the pupils have the language experience to recognize the convention being exploited.

To put *Prayer Before Birth* (Louis MacNeice) beside *The Unknown Citizen* (Auden) makes clear the range of language choice open to a poet. Locate the common ground between the two poems. Then explore how the different language of each works on the reader and causes him to see the common ground from a different angle. Describe the kind of language each uses, its source, the way it controls the reader's response. What frame of mind is caused by the literary echo in *Prayer Before Birth*, the low-key case-history manner of *The Unknown Citizen*? What kind of judgement does each prompt?

Another opportunity occurs with poems which set two kinds of language working against one another. For example, *A Fire Truck* (R. Wilbur). Two things happen: a roaring shining event outside and a quite secret jump in the poet's mind. How does the language make the reader know exactly what each event is like? Watch how action words and thought words quarrel throughout. Think of the fire truck and the poet as two characters arguing. What sort of voice has each? Which *fire* has not been extinguished at the end?

A more difficult example is *Naming of Parts* (Henry Reed). The poem demands maturity, but it does appear in anthologies intended for fourteen- to sixteen-year-olds and can be an extremely rewarding experience if the handling is as tactful as the poem is itself. The opposition of the instructor's naming of the parts of a gun and the poet's naming of the unperturbed life of the garden is immediately clear: the efficient weapon of destruction and the delicate machinery of growth. Pupils have no difficulty in recognizing the different idiom used for each part: for the instructor an apparently straightforward recording of everyday speech; for the garden the 'minutely appropriate words' of poetic language. Reason sees the opposition as obvious. What is imaginatively and emotionally shocking is the harmony within which the two parts exist. There is no dislocation: the same rhythm holds both with the same ease. Each comes out of a totally different belief in life, yet the two dance together as if they were natural partners. What kind of thinking does this prompt in the reader? What time is represented by *today*? Investigate the word *we* throughout. What question is the poem asking about

> . . . the point of balance,
> Which in our case we have not got . . .

Does the poem offer an answer? Young readers may or may not recognize the sexual implications, but the teacher needs to be ready to meet the recognition naturally. Embarrassed sniggering means that the readers are not mature enough for the experience, and if this is judged to be the likely outcome, it would be wiser not to attempt the poem at all.

Strange Meeting (Wilfred Owen) has a most compelling effect if it is introduced after experience of a number of poems which enact the physical and psychological horror of war. For example, *The Sentry*, *The Chances*, *Dulce et Decorum Est* (Wilfred Owen); *Attack*, *The Hero* (Siegfried Sassoon); *Landscape with Figures* (Keith Douglas); *The Battle* (Louis Simpson). In such a context young readers are caught by the surprise of *Strange Meeting*, disposed to share in the new silence, the withdrawal. They are usually ready to stay with the poem, to 'probe' with the poet the dark they find themselves in. Invite them to write down individually a sentence, a phrase, a word, to describe their first impression. Some typical responses are: it doesn't sound like a poem about war; silence, vagueness, a strange atmosphere; a hopeless feeling; it is old-fashioned, far away, not like a modern poem; I'm not sure what he is talking about; being in the dark place of the dead. These first impressions guide exploration of what the language of the poem is enacting. Remoteness: images and phrasing that strike the modern ear as belonging to another time. Silence and vagueness, the place of the dead: how is the reader made to imagine *the sullen hall*? Examine sounds as well as images. Notice the shadow effect of the escaping rhymes. It doesn't sound like a poem about war: Examine *Here is no cause to mourn*. What state does escape out of battle lead to? What do the dead soldiers bring with them? Explore the *hopelessness*, *the pity war distilled*. Notice how the negatives accumulate throughout the poem. How far does the vision of war reach? What has the remoteness of language to do with the reader's perception of this? What time do *enemy* and *friend* belong to? Is there only one war?

Examined fears

A number of the poems which pupils find in their anthologies make demands on their courage to face humanly the distorting human realities of pain, horror, death. The value of experience of such work is obvious in an environment where human viciousness is exploited as a source of entertainment. The 'video nasty' works by bludgeoning the receiver into suppressing his questioning, judging facility. The poem challenges him to think and feel as a moral being capable of choosing his attitude to the painful, the disturbing fact. In this connection, observing the craft of the challenge can have a positively supportive effect. The reason, I suggest, is that the exercise by involving the reader in the writer's control of the frightening reality helps him to discover his own power to control what at first sight seems intolerable. Paradoxically the experience is both distanced and brought closer. There is time for thinking and assimilating.

Hunting With a Stick (Michael Baldwin)
The shock the poem causes is the shock of recognizing a buried self. There is a natural recoil from the common paradox of childhood innocence and childhood cruelty, which shows itself in a desire to read the event as exceptional, in a condemnation of the child's *I wanted this death*. After the first exclamations and rejections, I should start examining how the poem makes the reader think again about the popular

image of young children. In the first stanza the child is behaving as children are expected to behave. Explore the expectations raised by the language: the tapping of reader-memory, the invitation to laughter, the way the relationship between child and rabbit is presented. The frost in the first stanza is just frost. How is it transferred and transformed in the second stanza? The language of the first stanza reflects the child's happy awareness of his surrounding. What happens to that awareness in the second stanza? How does the language convey the change? What happens to the reader's comfortable image of child and rabbit now? What sensation begins to work in the strange lines that close the stanza? In the third stanza feeling takes another lunge. The language concentrates on the mangled head of the rabbit. Yet the reader knows exactly what the child is feeling. How? Identify the relationship between child and rabbit at this point. The last stanza begins by releasing reader and rememberer from the experience, putting it at a distance. What has this to do with the effect of the last lines? Explore the shock of the alliteration in the last line. Explore how much work *my shadow falconed* is doing in making the reader share what the child understood. Examine the line-arrangement, the decreasing length of stanzas, the coming and going of rhyme across stanzas. How does this hold together the conflicting parts of the experience? How is the word *me* made to stand out alone? So what does it all mean? Does it stop at *ten years old*?

More Light! More Light! (Anthony Hecht)
Sharing the writer's effort to master the unendurable fact helps young readers to face this poem. Examine how the telling enacts the writer's painful struggle not to turn away, the sense of his forcing himself to stay among *those who were by*. That starting with a brutality from hundreds of years ago: why start at such a distance? Relate it to what follows. Watch the strain in the language. Starting from *we move now*, trace the conflict between a bare recording of facts in the idiom of everyday speech and a more heightened poetic manner. How does this compel the reader to share the poet's emotion, the war in heart and head. The form is the simplest of forms: four-line stanzas with the second and fourth lines rhyming. Connect this simplicity of form with what the poet is trying to do. Notice the clarity with which the event is made present. Set that against the incomprehensibility of what happens. Take *That shall judge all men* and pick up the word *judge*. Think of the poem as begging the reader to help in judgement. Is there any sure judgement? Examine the idea of 'light' in the poem. Give the readers the origin of the title: Goethe's reported last words, 'Mehr Licht! Mehr Licht!' Set the *howl* of the first event against the silence of the second. In the context of the whole poem think about the resonance of

'I implore my God to witness that I have made no crime'.

Where does the last stanza take writer and reader? Why should such a poem be written? Be read? Is there any hope?

Death in Leamington (Betjeman)
The barrier to be crossed is the barrier of irony. Recognition of irony and appreciation of the increase of meaning it makes possible demands a linguistic agility that develops gradually. Not surprisingly the subtler forms of irony disconcert young readers. They respond readily to irony which appeals to their sense of humour. Irony which appeals to their compassion is a stiffer challenge and it needs patience on our part to persuade them to the necessary thinking again. *Death in Leamington* can shock them by what appears to them as an unfeeling lightness of attitude to a pathetic subject. Start from that response. What causes it? What sort of verse does the poem remind them of? Generally, the fact that Betjeman borrows the form of hymns is recognized quickly. (If they are slow to see this, try chanting a couple of stanzas.) Someone may object that he is making fun of hymns. What bits are at the opposite pole from the kind of language we expect in a hymn? Is he really trying to be funny? Notice how he begins; the pity in the first two stanzas. So the shock doesn't come till the entry of the Nurse. How does the fact that we have first been moved increase the shock? What is it that shocks? Try changing the context: forget that the old woman has died. Now how does the behaviour of the Nurse strike us? What further cause for pity does it give in addition to pity at the lonely death? So the shock makes us know and feel more. How much does the poet blame the Nurse? Is it a condemnation of one callous person? Think about the last two stanzas. Now take up the stanza

> Do you know that the stucco is peeling?
>   Do you know that the heart will stop?
> From those yellow Italianate arches
>   Do you hear the plaster drop?

What feeling explodes in the poet's suddenly beginning to ask questions? Who is he addressing? The event is located in a certain kind of place and a certain style of living. How does this affect the reader's understanding? Pupils may take refuge in the unfamiliarity of the setting. I should not press the matter unless one of them points out that it is not only in Leamington that death can be like this.

Because I Could Not Stop for Death (Emily Dickinson)
The clear drama of Dickinson's poetry seldom fails to arrest the attention of young readers. The reason, I think, is the distinctive confidence of her diction, the absence of pressure on the reader to agree or disagree. They appear to feel free in her company. The ease comes perhaps from that quality of her seeming to speak from 'great streets of

silence'. So they accept her openness to the mystery of being as they accept her alertness to the natural world.

It is always worth first trying the strategy of standing aside from exploration of *Because I Could Not Stop for Death*, intervening very little until the exploration runs dry. The following is an outline of a fourth year class (average ability upwards) at work on the poem. Parenthesis indicates teacher intervention. There was the usual groping at first: It's about death—She's imagining her own funeral—The journey of the hearse—She doesn't seem to be afraid of dying. The exploration settled into a firmer direction when one member said, 'I don't think it's a funeral. There's no one else there, no mourners, no service. Death is driving the carriage. It's too quiet.'

— But it is a journey. It starts when Death stops the carriage and she gets in and they go on together to the house in the ground—the grave.
— Yes, the journey begins and ends. You can follow it step by step, past the school, past the fields of *gazing grain*, past the setting sun.
(How long does the journey take?)
— It's a whole day. The school is the morning, the fields the middle of the day, then the setting sun, the evening.
— It could be childhood, the school; adult, the middle of the day; old age, the setting sun.
— *The dews drew quivering and chill*. That makes you shiver. I think she's afraid there.
— When they reach the cemetery it's dark: *hardly visible*. That could be dying.
— I thought *hardly visible* meant the grave. *The cornice in the ground*. Only a small hump—you can hardly see it.
— That's the point. They come to the cemetery. It *is* a funeral.
(Start where the journey starts.)
— Death stops—how can Death stop?
— I think it means that death is always there. You don't think about it but he's there waiting. She couldn't stop to think about death.
— But Death isn't waiting. He's moving. He has to *stop* the carriage.
(Follow that line).
— Death is going on all the time . . .
— *Kindly*, like a friend giving a lift. She doesn't mind getting in. She doesn't mind putting away what she's doing. *I had put away my labour and my leisure too*.
— Immortality is in the carriage too . . . *Immortality* and *civility*—they rhyme.
(Does any other word rhyme with them?)
— *Eternity* at the end.
— I still think it's a funeral. It moves slowly like a funeral. There's a hearse and a grave.

(Look at the stanza *Or rather, he passed us*. *See* the image).

— Gossamer and tulle—that's not like a funeral. It's more like a summer dress. That makes you think of a happy time.
— Or a white wedding-dress, light and frilly.
— It could be about dying young.

(Does anyone else think that? General rejection on the grounds that the poem wasn't tragic enough.)

— We haven't looked at the last stanza where she seems to be still alive . . .
— What does it mean?
— *Surmised*—that means guessed, doesn't it. Not being sure, but guessing the meaning of something. Guessing the meaning of death. The carriage is going *towards Eternity*. Death is going to eternity . . .

Efforts to unknot the paradox of *'centuries shorter than a day'* ran into confused frustration, so the teacher took over to guide thinking. Three terms signifying time: *centuries*, *day*, *Eternity*. Sense in which *centuries* is being used: figuratively, to mean a great length of measurable time. Compare: It's ages since something or other happened. Sense in which *Eternity* is being used: literally, not figuratively, the word for un-measurable time, for timelessness. Between, the word *day*: the time of the writer's flash of perception of the reality of eternity. So ages of time seem shorter than the day of the vision when the writer 'saw' eternity.

The poem was read again to let the two journeys, the physical and the spiritual, come into focus. Then the craft was examined. How the verse enacts the physical journey, the regular pace of the lines enacting the slow steady advance of a horse-drawn carriage. How the physical journey enacts the spiritual journey: the sense of distance covered, the repetition of the word *passed* conveying a gradual withdrawal from the ordinary world and its affairs. Why the deliberate error about the sun's movement: *Or rather—he passed us*? *Or rather* draws attention to the error. From what perspective is it not an error? How does it make clearer the distance between ordinary knowledge and the extraordinary knowledge the writer is seeking to express? *The dews drew quivering and chill*: the only line to suggest fear. Is it only the words *quivering* and *chill* that enact fear? Listen to the halt in the movement of *The dews drew*—the only time the regular rhythm is broken. The repetition of *in the ground*. Awkward? Connection with the end of both journeys? The rhyme *immortality*, *civility*, *Eternity* comes at the beginning and at the end. What vision of death is being uncovered as the poem grows?

The biography of a poem

The work described in this section is a first step towards as full a description of a poem as readers are capable of. It is intended for fourth and fifth year pupils who have a fair experience of poetry and who have over the years acquired some knowledge of how a poem lives. The aim is to train pupils in bringing together knowledge already gained bit by bit. Everything the readers know is brought to bear on observation of a short poem.

The principle of approach is that since a work of art has a distinctive life, a distinctive way of existing, a 'biography' can be put together by the reader who interrogates it, a biography, that is, of the *poem*, not of the poet. The 'biographers' are concerned only with what the poem on the page has to tell them about itself.

There are three stages in the work, each of which starts with a reading aloud of the poem. The first stage is undirected investigation, the pupils working in small groups. The second stage is a pooling and development of the findings of the first stage, the teacher now being the leader. The third stage is getting the biography into coherent shape. The work takes from two to four periods, depending on the poem and the stamina of the biographers. The second stage takes longest, particularly with bright classes who are less likely to be quickly satisfied. An advantage of the exercise is the amount of rereading and rethinking generated; this reinforces the lesson that in a poem every word demands attention and corrects the tendency to read with a wandering eye.

The work is oral, including the final shaping which is recorded only in a communal draft. It is important not to imply that there is a fixed formula for the third stage. The shape of a biography varies from poem to poem. Biographers may decide to start with first impression or last impression; they may decide to work out from what they feel to be the centre of the poem or to follow the growth of the poem in sequence; they may decide to use the shape of their own gradual discovery. Openness helps to prevent falling into stereotyped habits in individual written work.

A Poison Tree (Blake) fourth year class

First stage

The class had met the poem in the first year and many of them knew it by heart. They were prompted to take their previous experience into account and see if time had changed their response.

Second stage

Points brought forward from the first stage: all groups reported a change in response, generally agreeing that they took the poem more seriously now. They were struck by things they hadn't thought of before: the extraordinariness of using a simple story about apple-stealing to express the results of secret anger, the oddity of sunning anger with smiles and watering it with tears. The second stanza had clearly taken up much of the group discussion. All groups had related the poem to their own experience of how a secret grudge strengthens, of the patience and hypocrisy it leads to. *The apple bright* was connected with the tree in Eden and the temptation of Eve. One group also drew in Snow White's apple, because of the word 'poison' in the title. The apple was taken to stand for temptation. Comments on craft: simple, dramatic, saying a great deal in a small space; repetition of *night* and *morning* conveying the obsession of the speaker; from one group the observation that the emphasis on the repeated *and* gave the impression of gloating.

Points developed: word 'simple' considered and discarded as unsuitable on the grounds that there was too much going on beneath the words and that the story was too extraordinary. Investigation of the idea 'extraordinary' posed new questions. Readers moved from the extraordinary idea of wrath growing into a tree to the perception that the image of open air growth strengthened the reader's sense of the inner destruction it stood for. Prompted to look at the shape of the poem, they saw how the close rhyming, the straight sentences, the repetitions (particularly of the word *and*) enacted the imprisonment of the speaker in his wrath.

The *apple bright* image was explored. This time the idea that it stood for temptation was disputed. Hatred, evil, deceit were suggested. Eventually the image was taken as carrying all the suggestions, including temptation, on the grounds that the apple tempted the foe. This led to discussion of the place of the foe in the story: the knot of relationship between two persons, each guilty of trying to destroy the other. The word *glad* was examined. What charge does it carry? The foe is destroyed, the speaker victorious: is the speaker free of his hatred?

Attention was drawn to the first stanza, so far ignored. Observation showed that the repetitions started then. Prompting led to recognition of the connection between the repetition of *I* and the poison in the soul destroying speaker as well as foe. Further observation revealed the dominance of the sound *i* throughout, occurring in every line, and six times in a rhyming position. The difference between the literal statement of the first stanza and the metaphorical statement of the rest of the poem was noticed and added to the list of extraordinary things.

Third stage

Draft record: it was decided to start with the extraordinariness, then to deal with meaning, then with the language. Extraordinariness: anger with a foe which is not told turns into a tree, which bears an apple, which tempts the foe to steal it, which destroys the foe, which makes the owner glad.

Meaning: tackling this led to further understanding. Readers started with the plain first stanza and now noticed that there are two kinds of anger involved: the kind that can be told and is harmless; the kind that has its root in hatred. The poem shows the effects of the second kind.

The *apple bright* was now seen as primarily the evil of hatred; the temptation association became less important. Hatred, the foe's as well as the speaker's. His gladness is itself evil.

The charge of the language: strong feeling is conveyed by being packed into short lines, short familiar words. Every word, however simple, is important. Rhymes and repetitions compel the reader to listen. He is trapped by the speed with which the wrath of the first stanza becomes a story of secret poison, and so is tempted by the shining apple. It is only when he stands back from the poem that he sees the danger.

The Fisherman (Yeats)

First stage

The Fisherman is a good demonstration of how a poem can create its own context so fully that the reader does not require specialized knowledge to participate and understand. There is no need to provide information about Irish history. The poem is complex but it is a stimulating challenge for readers who enjoy using their heads. The account that follows is drawn from the work of different fifth year classes and is fairly representative of how, in my experience, pupils engage with the poem. Initial group exploration produces an amount of disagreement and usually takes a full period.

Second stage

Points of disagreement—subject: about his poetry not being listened to; about indifference to art and poetry; about the kind of poetry he wants to write; about political corruption; about love of country. Tone and feeling: scornful, angry, sad, idealistic, cynical. The fisherman: a real man the poet has seen, a man he has invented; stands for the kind of audience he wants, stands for what he thinks everyone should be.

Development: The aim is not to get rid of disagreement but to recognize diversity as true to the poem, to test the validity of different responses. Reflection shows that subject, feeling, tone are as complex as the different suggestions imply. The charge of cynicism is usually a source of hot argument and leads to a more precise identification of what some readers dislike about the poem; the sense that it is élitist and has no room for the hopes of ordinary people. This leads to examining the figure of the fisherman, the figure holding the complexity together. Is the fisherman actual or imagined? Notice how he first appears, the sharp-edged details which make him visible. Most readers agree that at first they take him as actual. *I can see him still* and *call up to the eye* imply remembering rather than inventing. It is later that doubt enters. *Imagining a man* inclines the reader to think he is an invention. The impression appears to be confirmed by

> A man who does not exist,
> A man who is but a dream.

But is the statement literal or ironic—a way of emphasizing the collapse of the poet's hopes, his disillusionment? Notice how the fisherman gains in vitality at his second appearance by being seen against the background of *this audience*. The interesting thing is that the *audience* is actual: the clue is there in the way the list starts; not with type figures but with people the poet could name. Examine the visibility of fisherman and the characters in the audience, the kind of detail used in each. Especially the effect of that single gesture, *the down turn of his wrist*. Again, the fisherman has a landscape to move in. What about the audience? Which has the more substance, fisherman or audience?

Most pupils see the fisherman as both actual and imagined, a fictional figure taken from actual experience. Whether individual readers take him as this or not, these all agree that he represents something other than himself, as the members of the audience do not. As the poem grows so does the significance of the fisherman. At the end of the poem two ideals come together in the figure, an ideal of poetry and an ideal of community. But can the fisherman be taken as the actual audience the poet wants? Is there anything at all to suggest that Yeats thinks of the fisherman as actually reading his poems? Examine the two pairs of words: *wise and simple, cold and passionate*. How do they lead the reader to understand the relation of fisherman to poet?

Wise and simple. Observe how the image of the fisherman controls the kind of language used: the easy fit of *Maybe, twould be, a twelve month since, grey Connemara cloth* . . . An interesting effect of the poem is that readers take the craft for granted. It is usually only when prompted that they notice the mastery which makes finding rhymes appear an easy matter. It was Yeats who exhorted his fellow-poets, 'Learn your trade', and who wanted 'a speech so natural and dramatic that the hearer would feel the presence of a man thinking and feeling'(**29**). Judge him by his own standards. Is there a false note? What about

> The beating down of the wise
> And great Art beaten down

Usually there are two views about these lines: that they are vague and spoil the naturalness by drawing attention to themselves; that it is right to shout down the *audience* with this boom before returning to the quietness of the fisherman. Connect the movement of the poem with the fisherman *climbing up to a place*. The rhythm does enact a steady walking-pace. Notice that the only check comes near the end in

> I shall have written him one
> Poem maybe . . .

Third stage

A Description of the advance of the poet's thinking in the order the poem follows: clear image of a fisherman moving through grey hills at dawn; poet linking the image with his desire to write for his own people. Word *reality* releases a contrasting image of very different men; frustration expressed in scornful account of audience whose values the poet despises. Turns away from an audience which rejects wisdom and art to the fisherman who now is seen as illusion. Description of the kind of poetry the poet wanted to write.

B   Image of fisherman: both expressing the poet's values and controlling the way the poem is written.

C   Reader and poem: reaction of reader to voice of poem; to the values expressed.

5
'The bread of faithful speech'

(Wallace Stevens)

Talking about a work of art is a natural result of the experience itself, of the energy released by the charge of the work. There is an urge to tell others of what excites pleasure and interest, to share new ideas, new questions that the work provokes. An element in the impulse is that talking about art allows a kind of communication about the inexpressible, about what is most of the time trapped beneath ordinary discourse. Shared collaboration deepens and extends individual response; our hold on the work is strengthened by showing it to others and being shown it by them. Writing about the experience is another form of collaboration, much more difficult, which most of us seldom engage in. We set our pupils to that, as we set them to write about other kinds of experience, as an essential means of development of their language power.

Writing about poetry is difficult, but not more so than writing about any other vivid experience. The writer is on his own without the support of others to fill in the gaps in his capacity to find words for half-realized ideas and feelings. There is value in the withdrawal involved—an opportunity to reflect on personal relationship with the new item in the mindscape. Writing about it demands a concentration of effort, the reward of which is a better understanding of what one knows and feels. The effort can bring the writer closer to the work; can sometimes result in a further insight. Our job is to make sure that the effort looked for really is matched to the present capacity of the writers, that the kind of writing asked for is not so unattractive a task that the pleasure of the poem is dimmed in the effort. We need to be clear about what can be reasonably expected at different stages of growth. Above all, we need to be clear that the value of the exercise depends on its being a genuinely personal act, an account of what a given writer thinks, feels, observes. The capacity to respond to poetry cannot be systematized into a neat progression, but the ability to articulate response can be seen as having definable stages. We can say that there are different exercises appropriate at different levels. We cannot teach delight, but we can teach some of the ways of writing about the object that causes delight.

Most of us are familiar with the difference between the quick satisfaction we sense in oral collaboration and the trudging written comment that follows. There is always a gap between what children recognize intuitively and what they can express in writing. However wide the gap, what they can manage to write is a valuable kind of collaboration worth encouraging. Teaching them to write is a matter of the art of the possible.

Parallel poets

The first stage is writing not directly about a poem, but out of a poem, when the experience leads to a parallel imaginative act. Poems, like music, pictures, sensory objects, are used as a starting-point for independent creative activity. Readers will be familiar with several excellent books which describe ways of stimulating pupils to make the effort of catching experience in 'the cool web of language' (**25**). Whatever material is used as a stimulus, it is poetry which is the teacher, which shows the way, by providing experience of the possibilities of play with language. Again, the dynamism of language in a poem can release a dynamism in the children's language. Someone has said that it is enough that a poet should build us his world, which is precisely what we hope for when we encourage children to write poetry.

Writing out of a poem is writing about poetry in the sense that it is writing about the imaginative activity the poem causes. Besides being a valuable way of stimulating creative action, the practice fosters acceptance of poems as natural objects in the landscape which take their place with other familiar experiences. Further, when what follows a poem is a personal imaginative effort, the right foundation is being laid for later writing directly about poetry. What is being implicitly established is the importance of an intuitive connection with the poem; a connection that is primary at any level of reflection. For this reason, the linking of poetry and free writing shold not be confined, as it often is, to the junior years. Certainly, the most lively results come from first and second year pupils when the writing often has both the freshness of childhood and the dawning consciousness of adolescence. Efforts can show a moving confidence, which comes perhaps from their not yet having realized how uncomfortable consciousness can be. This is particularly noticeable in the work of slower pupils. In the early secondary years it is frequently these pupils who produce the best work in this area. They are less prone to the derivativeness, the attempt at pastiche that brighter children show at this stage. The success is of inestimable value in countering the boredom and misery, the failure that education too often means for the non-academic pupil. To produce a piece of work clearly worthy of general admiration can have also most heartening side-effects. I remember one struggling twelve-year-old who broke through an apparently insurmountable difficulty with writing of any kind as a result of success in writing a poem.

The pastiche that brighter children incline towards is of course natural and is not pastiche to them. Imitation is a way of learning a craft and a signal of collaboration with the masters. It is often children with some flair for writing who are drawn towards imitation. There is something to be said for occasionally setting a bright group to deliberate pastiche. The exercise sharpens attention to the features of the original, but it is, in my view, of limited value as a method of stimulating the effort of finding words for what the young writer alone knows. Remarkable results can be achieved, but there is a danger in the remarkableness. In young writings, awkwardness is a truer signal of intense effort than mandarin fluency.

Readiness to choose verse as a means of expression usually declines in the middle years. There are a number of possible reasons. The decline may be the result of the option of using verse not being made explicitly available by the teacher. But it is probably also a natural development, the result of increasing critical powers which make pupils less ready to think that they can write verse. It may also be a quite natural reserve of confidence, a claim to privacy. They may not choose to write poetry because they recognize how revealing a poem can be. It might be more accurate to say that they do not choose to offer poetry to an audience. There is probably more secret writing than we ever suspect. Whatever the reason, creative activity in the middle years is more likely to show itself in the more manageable medium of prose. There is of course no point in demanding that pupils should write poems for us. The instruction 'write a poem' can be as paralyzing as the instruction 'write a composition'. In this kind of writing, the writers should be perfectly free to choose the form themselves. What we are hoping for, after all, is not a set of poems for the school magazine, but that the learners should sometimes reach as high as their own ceiling of saying. If the choice of medium is truly their choice, they are more likely to find what Wallace Stevens calls 'the bread of faithful speech'. What matters is the degree of attention brought to the work, not the form it takes.

Pleasurable experience of poetry, increasing ability in active reception, interest in the attentiveness of craft in a poem: it is these things which nourish the kind of effort hoped for. The real successes are always unpredictable and surprising. They may not, for instance, bear the usual marks of 'creative' writing at all. On one occasion in the middle of a poetry lesson with a second year group of average to high ability, a large red leaf floated in through the open window. The room was on the third floor and the appearance of the leaf was surprising enough to take up the rest of the lesson. Later the event was set as a writing topic. The results were satisfactory in that different children handled the task in different ways: some attempted description of the way the leaf floated in, or of the leaf itself; some focused on the surprise of the event, or on the contrast between the leaf and the classroom; some speculated about the journey of the leaf; some used the leaf as a metaphor. About half the class used verse as a medium. One pupil chose an unexpected way of handling the task, a way completely independent of anything that had happened in the classroom talk about the event:

'During English class we were discussing the different ways that Matthew Arnold and Thomas Hardy looked at nature (**30**). Matthew Arnold thinks more of the way the beauty of the country can be imitated in a little park in the centre of London, and the surface beauty of nature, not the deep mystery that surrounds natural beauty. He thinks that man knows so much about nature that he can make an exact copy of it. Thomas Hardy thinks more of the mystery and wonder of nature, which he shows in his poem. He knows that though man can make artificial things to make life comfortable, he can never recreate the beauty and wonder of nature, of the shy curiosity of the fallow deer peeping in the curtains to gaze at the artificiality of the house and its contents.

As if to prove the point, a leaf drifted in the window, lovely and red, tinged with the colours of autumn. Who could make anything like it?'

What is striking there is the unusual maturity of imagination, the thinking which perceived a relationship between different elements of the experience. It is a genuinely creative act, even though it does not conform to the usual expectations of creative writing.

Writing about poetry: first stage

'It's as if he didn't say it out loud'.
'When I was reading it I thought I was the only person in the world who knew about it'.
'I heard a sort of quietness except at the end where it's like a choir singing'.

Three written comments by first year pupils on the carol *I sing of a maiden*, set as an unseen at an end of term test, in response to the instruction: Read the poem trying to hear it in your head. What do you hear? The comments were made by children of very different academic ability(**31**). (The spelling of one has been corrected.)

The interest for our purpose is that—like the lines William Spouge's pupil drew through *Flying Crooked* (p.40)—such comments tell us what children can actually do. When a poem has caught their imagination, they are capable of finding a way to record the impression that other readers recognize as true and valid. Modern criticism finds impressionistic response unsatisfactory: intuitive comment gives an inadequate account of the art. But it is in subjective impression and intuition that objective criticism begins. 'Unless what we describe is capable of being felt intuitively, there would be no point in describing it'(28). In the classroom, the feeling intuitively is of prime importance, the foundation that needs to be firmly established before there is any question of training in more objective description. It would be a mistake to try to impose an objective approach on minds whose response is still naturally subjective. Too early a demand for objective comment weakens the pupils' confidence in the value of their own response and leads to their taking refuge in the stereotyped glibness they find in examination aids and notes.

The problem is to find ways of tapping the imaginative energy released by the poem which do not smack of routine poetry exercises, which do not give the notion that writing about poetry is a matter of learning and applying formulae. Variety is important, a certain unpredictability in the way writing is invited. We need to aim at a lively concreteness and to avoid giving instructions in general terms. Young learners are vulnerable to the influence of the abstract or general term for the very reason that it is alien to the way their minds actually work. Thus, it is not enough to tell them to write what impression a poem makes on them. Just as we seek to match presentation to the particular poem, so we should seek to match the written exercise to the particular experience. The way writing is invited aims at refreshing experience of the poem; causing a new contact with it, strengthening trust in the value of imaginative intuitive response. The instruction to read *I sing of a maiden* 'trying to hear it in your head' aimed at drawing attention to the stillness enacted in the language. The children were not told that it had this quality; the results showed that they were perfectly capable of discovering this for themselves. The instruction matched that poem; it would not match every poem. Impressionistic writing about poetry can be invited in the junior years whenever we can think of the right question. Such work is best done in class, when interest is fresh and attention undistracted. It is not always easy to think of a way of tapping imaginative energy. When inspiration fails us, it is better not to look for written work at all.

Chapters 2 and 3 contain a number of suggestions for work of this kind, ways of accustoming pupils to writing about poetry as a manageable activity which does not require learning a new language. Some of the suggestions for oral collaboration can also be adapted to written work. For example, the connections started up by a poem might be written rather than spoken.

The intention of a written exercise is to establish the habit of exploring personal possession of a poem, discovering how it lives in the imagination of a reader. A simple exercise is a written version of what is happening in a poem which the children have heard but not seen. There is no preliminary discussion. A starting sentence is given. For example: Three people are waiting on a platform for a train (*At the Railway Station*   Hardy). A chimney sweeper in the days when children were used for cleaning chimneys is thinking about his life (*The Chimney Sweeper*   Blake). A child is riding in a waggon with her grandfather (*Manners*   Elizabeth Bishop). *It was time for the mare to foal* (*Birth of a foal*   Ferenc Juhasz). A bullfight starts. The bull is released (*Bullfight*   Miroslav Holub). The children need to listen to the poem a few times before writing. An advantage of the poem not being seen is that there is a better chance of the experience being taken as a whole. The writers are not distracted by difficulties in the language and are saved from the awkwardness of 'The poet says—next he says—then he says' formula. Instead they are likely to absorb into their own writing elements which attract them.

Another possibility with poems which relate an incident is to go beyond the story to what happened next. What happened when the children had gone home? (*Poor Old Guy*   Walter de la Mare) What happened to the foal when the two people had continued their journey? (*The Runaway*   Robert Frost) (One twelve-year-old's account contained the sentence; He sinks down in the cold, struggling weakly, his hooves *grasping* the air. An example of how poetry can inspire writers to find the right word.) What would you put under the tree? (*How to Paint a Perfect Christmas*   Miroslav Holub) What happens between the two stanzas of *Take One Home for the Kiddies* (Philip Larkin)? In this work the children are free to use any form they wish. They are not required to write another stanza. Generally, they write better when they are not trying to use the verse-form of the original.

Another method is to send the readers behind the poem to the raw material which caused it. On one occasion a second year lower stream class were clearly moved by *Vergissmeinicht* (Keith Douglas). They were asked to put themselves in the position of being the poet writing a letter to someone close to him to whom he describes the incident, and to write that part of the letter which contained the description. There were signs of real engagement in the results, many of which were marked by a rhythm of language matching the rhythm of their feeling. For example, one pupil wrote: 'Well, yesterday he was moad down. And lying in the battlefield surrounded in dry blood, which once trickled from his body, I say a picture of a girl, and on the back, was written Steffi Vergissmeinicht. His arms lay beside him waiting to be used. But he no longer lived, to use them. His eyes were closed. And he lay there with pain in his eyes. But the girl in the picture, would weep and die to see her lover shoot down in such a dedly manner'.

Another possibility is a letter to a poet, present or past, suggesting a subject for a new poem, the suggestion being inspired by an actual poem which has caught the letter-writer's interest. An advantage of such exercises is that the poet ceases to be a textbook enemy. For older pupils an exercise which helps to reinforce the reader/poet dialogue is the letter from reader to poet about his poem. Readers write as stranger or personal friend, express satisfaction or dissatisfaction, ask for confirmation of meaning or ask for explanation of something they don't understand. The pressure of having to explain is removed; the poet is an audience who can be taken to understand what he has written. Difficulties become questions rather than threats to self-esteem; the poem is allowed its mystery.

Another way of stirring readers to examine their experience of a poem is to set them to discover the further independent thoughts it sets going. This works well with poems which do not reveal themselves plainly or which confront the reader with the uncommon. *The North Ship* (see chapter 3) is an example. To free readers from the influence of communal reaction they are asked to look at the poem again, rather as they would look at a picture, letting different bits catch their attention —not, that is, to start reading it through. There is no question of the thinkers being required to show a connection between their thoughts and the poem. Thoughts of individual readers may have no obvious connection with the poem at all. Or they may throw new light on the poem for other readers. For example, *Snow* (Louis MacNeice) provoked in one reader the thought of 'all that goes on under the skin of the fruit'. This led the class to the perception that the poem is about all that goes on under the skin of the world.

An end-of-term project which makes revision interesting is making maps or guides. The poetry read during the term is thought of as forming a country or city. A map is made in which the different poems are identified as places of interest, for example: Good Walking Country, Story-teller's Circle, Accident Black Spot, Hawk Seen Here, Joke Shop, Museum, Singing Nightly, Observatory. Places are numbered and a key is provided giving the title of relevant poems. Thus Museum would refer map-users to poems about life in the past, Joke-Shop would refer them to humorous poems, and so on. Map-makers are free to make any connections they wish; links do not have to be thematic. *Frogs* (Norman McCaig) and *The Squire* (Chaucer) might find themselves side by side in an Art Gallery on the grounds of their strong visual quality. *Birth of a Foal* (Ferenc Juhász) and *The Fly* (Blake) might find themselves together in Viewing Point as unusual ways of seeing things.

Dullness and derivativeness in writing about poetry is the result of pupils not trusting what they know personally. The intention in this first stage is to establish firmly the value of personal impression; not the first vague impression, but the deeper impression that comes with the re-thinking involved in the challenge to write it down. Impressionistic comment should have a place at any level; it remains the necessary starting-point of more formal reflection.

Formal comment: teaching the elements

It is wise not to begin training in formal comment until pupils are at ease with the kind of written work described in the previous section. Generally, the third year is time enough. What is involved is not initiation into the language of professional criticism, but learning to record what the young reader can notice and understand. As in earlier writing, the implicit assumption is that the pupils already have enough language at their disposal to do the job—as indeed they have. We are not looking for a borrowed glibness, but for a gradually increasing ability to articulate actual observation.

Pupils acquire a language for writing about poetry in the intersubjective exchange of oral collaboration. The quality of the talk influences the quality of the writing. The teacher is a key participant whose language is naturally of great importance. The less stereotyped it is, the less danger there is of the children's being stereotyped. Written collaboration has its source in oral collaboration, but the two kinds involve, of course, two different ways of using language. The act of writing always involves a remove. To write demands a mastery of conventions other than those involved in speech, and we need to give deliberate attention to the remove from speech to writing, to give enough time to the elements of translating the spurts and gestures of talk into written form. It is a matter of avoiding at one extreme educating pupils in the clichés of lit.crit. and at the other leaving them to flounder in the casual incoherence of speech. A full transcript of a class talking about a poem will show the normal untidiness of spoken dialogue: the hesitations, 'sort-ofs', questions, sentence-fragments, the sudden flashes, the doubling back, the lurches away from the poem, the line of exploration that leads to understanding and the line that leads nowhere. When a poem catches fire, a great deal of thinking and feeling takes place, very much more than most pupils can turn into writing. Some of it—the most important part for pupils as for all readers—lies too deep for expression. Our concern in written work is the expressible part. The written exercise guides the pupil towards saying the sayable out of the volume of ideas he has encountered.

The important word is 'guides'. The teacher's behaviour is a crucial factor in classroom reception; his invisible support is just as necessary in the distractions of the livingroom. Only the teacher knows what has actually happened during a lesson, and his question is a direct link with that. A teacher's question is more likely to be successful, for instance, than the question in the book, if the book contains questions. Again, it is important to avoid general questions which might apply to any poem. Questions or instructions need to be precise in intention and to remind the reader of what he knows. *Explain* and *say why* are slippery instructions which should be used with caution. They may be asking the impossible. It is possible for a reader to explain what he understands by a line or a word. It is notoriously difficult to explain sensations of pleasure. Pupils can say that such and such pleases them in a poem, but they cannot explain why, any more than they can explain why they like the colour red or the taste of coffee. Instructions for written work need to help the pupil to write, not merely tell him to do so. The questions we set are a teaching, not a testing, instrument; a way of focusing attention and making sure the pupils have to hand necessary structures and items of vocabulary. It is through the way written work is set, for instance, that terms used in oral work gradually become part of the children's writing vocabulary. Again, the instructions are themselves models of the move from speech to writing in that they are written versions of our speech during a lesson.

Time and practice are needed if pupils are to master the elements of formal description. The skill to be taught is description of what can be observed and thus described: aspects of meaning and craft. It is important that exercises should be short and manageable. Description of the observable is the more easily mastered if the amount is limited and the aspect clearly indicated. A written exercise does not try to cover all that has happened during oral collaboration but selects a single item. Besides developing the habit of close attention to the text, such exercises are a first step in training pupils to make draft notes of what they think as they read. It is essential to make sure that the children know the conventions for presenting quotation and reference and that they use them. The number of college students who appear to be ignorant of such matters suggests that they are not given enough attention in school. Yet the conventions are easy to teach and satisfying to learn. It is not enough to give oral instructions; examples of layout need to be demonstrated on the blackboard or overhead projector.

Very straightforward exercises are set at first to give practice in using the conventions. One simple form is recording the connection between the words in a poem and the feeling or mood conveyed to the reader. Part of the explorations suggested in chapters 3 and 4, for example, can become material for a written record. In chapter 3, examples are the isolation of words in *Mouse's Nest* which make the reader see clearly; the words in the first stanza of *To Autumn* which give the reader a feeling of richness brimming over; the image words and voice-over in *Pike*. In chapter 4, the relationship between *Whip lash* and other items in the poem; images in *The Darkling Thrush* which convey Hardy's mood. Another straightforward exercise is describing an obvious figure of sound which has been observed in oral collaboration: the shape of a stanza, a pattern of rhyme, echo or repetition, the sound value of a word, and so on. The purpose is to give practice in using certain tools for expression of observation.

Some sample questions and answers

The Squire (Chaucer)
What makes you know that Chaucer likes watching the Squire?
Mostly Chaucer likes looking at the Squire on his horse, he is so fresh and strong in his bright clothes:

> . . . *embroidered* like a meadow *bright*
> And full of *freshest* flowers, red and white.

He likes the Squire's happiness:

> Singing he was or fluting *all the day.*

He laughs at him a bit when he says the Squire is so fond of making love that

> He slept as little as a nightingale.

Hares at Play (John Clare)
Clare uses hardly any punctuation, only two dashes. How does he manage to be clear? Notice the kind of sentence he uses and the way the scene grows? Why does he use the two dashes?
Clare does not need full stops or commas because he goes from one thing to another without interrupting himself. He doesn't use complicated sentences. The first line

> The birds are gone to bed the cows are still

is just two simple sentences side by side.
He describes what he sees bit by bit. First the end of the day, then the hares playing until they hear *the milking maidens*, then the hares disappearing. You always know exactly what he is describing. When he is talking about the hares playing, you know *they* means the hares. Then he brings in the milkmaids so he uses the word *hare* again—*each nimbling hare*—when he brings back the hares.
In the line

> Sturts quick as fear—and seeks its hidden lair

the dash gives the impression of the hare stopping quickly. I don't think there is any need for the dash in

> Like toil a resting—lies the fallow plough.

Upon the Snail (Bunyan)
Whether you like snails or not, you don't think about that when you are reading the poem. What persuades you to forget about liking or not liking them? Notice the words used and the way the poem moves.
I don't like snails but I don't think about that when I am reading the

poem because there is nothing about snails being slimy and destroying plants. The only thing the poet talks about is how softly and surely they go. The words *softly*, *sure*, *makes no noise*, *still*, *quietly*, keep me thinking about this. *Softly* and *sure* are repeated. So is the word *go*.

The poem moves like the snail, softly and sure. The lines don't stumble. The word *stumble* made me realize that snails can't stumble, so a snail is a good image for doing things quietly and steadily.

During Wind and Rain (Hardy)

What has stanza shape to do with the reader's feeling aware of the two times in the poem? Describe the shape. How does rhyme hold the double pictures together? Notice that the tense is always present.

Each stanza has two parts. The first five lines describe a scene of happy family life. The second line of this part always has the same shape and ends with the word *yea* or *aye*:

> He, she, all of them—yea . . .
> Elders and juniors—aye . . .
> Men and maidens—yea . . .
> He, she, all of them—aye . . .

The last two lines of a stanza describe a scene of *wind and rain*. The first of these is always either

> Ah no; the years O!

or

> Ah no; the years, the years.

The tense in both parts is always present but it is not the same time. The last two lines make the reader aware that the family scene can't stay present. *The years* changes it to the past.

The first line of a stanza always rhymes with the last: *songs*, *throngs*; *moss*, *across*; *all*, *wall*; *house*, *ploughs*. This makes you feel that the family scenes are present only because they are in the poet's memory. Another thing that holds the two parts together and makes you aware of the two different times is the words *yea* or *aye* in the first part and the word *no* in the second.

The Wild Swans at Coole (Yeats)

Notice how many times in the poem Yeats uses a word which has the same shape as the word *autumn*: two syllables with the stress on the first. What do you notice about where they occur? How do these words affect the way you hear the poem?

Words that have the same shape as *autumn*:

Stanza 1   *Autumn, beauty, woodland, twilight, water, mirror, brimming, water, fifty*

Stanza 2   *nineteenth, autumn, finished, scatter, wheeling, broken*

Stanza 3   *brilliant, creatures, hearing, twilight, lighter*

Stanza 4   *lover, lover, paddle, passion, conquest, wander*

Stanza 5   *water, rushes*

Sometimes the words are side by side: *autumn beauty, water mirror, brimming water, nineteenth autumn, scatter wheeling, brilliant creatures, conquest, wander.*

Sometimes they have the same sound: *autumn, water, conquest, wander. Water, mirror, scatter, lover* end with the same sound.

I think these words are what makes the poem musical; in a way they are like the sound of the swans' wings:

> The *bell-beat* of their wings above my head.

There are nine of these words in the first stanza and only two in the last. This gives the feeling of the swans having *flown away*.

Draft work: second stage

The short exercise on a single aspect of the poem is the first step in the skill of keeping a draft record, in that emphasis is on the particular observation rather than on the general impression. At this stage, the method of answering is largely discursive; the writers use sentences rather than identify ideas by phrase or heading. It is easier for them since it is what they are used to doing. How not to use sentences and still be clear is a more sophisticated skill which has to be taught deliberately. The act of identifying and naming involved is of course essential to the development of thinking and writing power in any area of learning.

There are a number of reasons for teaching pupils to keep a draft record of their reading of poetry. The records naturally vary in quality and quantity, but all pupils benefit from the effort at precision the work demands. It is a more profitable method than the essay-type assignment. For the inexperienced thinker the weakness of the essay assignment on a poem is that it starts at the end of the process rather than at the beginning, puts the emphasis on bringing ideas together rather than on letting the ideas themselves become clear. The draft assignment puts the emphasis on the ideas. By removing the pressure to produce a piece of work 'finished' in the conventional sense of the essay, it removes the temptation to escape into generalities to fill up the page. It keeps the act of writing firmly linked to the act of reading. Thinking about a poem is of its nature an untidy process which does not advance in a neat sequence. There is a constant backtracking as the reader looks again at the text: he discovers that first thoughts about this or that won't do; some other element of the pattern springs into relief; the poem grows or shrinks the more it is looked at. Backtracking is unacceptable in an essay; it is a virtue in a draft record. Again, the approach means that there is always room for the reader to say what he wants to say rather than what the essay topic restricts him to saying. This is one reason why pupils tackle draft work more willingly and confidently than they do conventional questions. In this kind of work the writer is competing only with himself; he is not discouraged by vague notions of what 'they' expect him to say, by the belief that there is an ideal answer to measure himself by. Another reason for the willingness is the satisfaction of visible achievement—the professional look of a record folder or notebook. It is not only, then, that draft work provides plenty of practice in writing things down, and that it is necessary preparation for writing a coherent account of thinking. It is more than practice or preparation—an activity of irreplaceable value in itself, which should in my view form the bulk of written work on poetry in the fourth, fifth and sixth form.

Draft record of oral collaboration

A way of starting is to make a communal draft record of oral collaboration, with the blackboard serving as a model page. The class retraces the progress of discussion. Usually the sequence is accurately remembered, but this is unimportant. Items are recorded in the order in which they are recalled. Then the items are matched and grouped under identifying headings. For example, a draft record of the exploration of *Because I Could Not Stop for Death* (see chapter 4) would be arrived at like this:

Sequence of oral collaboration
About death, or a funeral, death driving the hearse. Journey takes a whole day. Day represents a lifetime. Fear in the line *The dews drew quivering and chill*. *Hardly visible*—the grave or dying. Meaning of Death *stops*. Death *kindly*; writer doesn't mind putting away life. Rhyme across poem: *immortality*, *civility*, *Eternity*. *Gossamer and tulle*—not like a funeral. Difficulty of last stanza. Pace of lines matches movement of carriage. Physical journey and spiritual journey. Oddity of *Or rather—he passed us*. Halt in rhythm—*The dews drew*. Repetition of *in the ground*. Writer's vision of death.

Grouping and identification
Subject   Death
Central image   Journey in a carriage. The driver (Death) stops to take up a passenger (the writer).
Development of journey image   Journey takes from morning (the school children playing *at recess*) to evening (*The dews* drew quivering and chill).

Physical journey expresses journey spirit takes with Death. Sense of great distance covered is conveyed (a) by places passed—school, fields, sky with *setting sun*; (b) by contrast between *day* and *centuries* in last stanza; (c) by *The Horses' heads were toward Eternity*. Sun moving past earth conveys how far beyond earth the travellers go.

Details of journey: children playing, crops ripening, setting sun: Journey of life from childhood to old age?

Rhythm: lines move to rhythm of comfortable journey in a carriage—*no haste*, Only one jolt—*The dews drew*—as carriage comes to a halt.

Other features that make the reader think

The carriage: First impression a hearse. But Death stops it *kindly*. Writer glad to get in, attracted by *his civility*. Carriage holds *immortality*, not mortality. *Gossamer and tulle*: suggest a different kind of journey, a wedding perhaps.

The grave is a *house*, a place to live in.

In the ground. Journey ends *in the ground*—life ends in the grave. But repetition makes reader think again. Does ending *in the ground* mean *ending*? The other passenger is *immortality*.

Vision of death. Extraordinary vision of death. Not sad or frightening, but friendly, natural. Gradual change from naturalness of first three stanzas to strangeness of last two. *Surmised*—wondering. Whole poem wondering about mystery of death. Rhyme—*immortality*, *civility*, *Eternity*—holds life and death together as if there was no break, just one natural journey to eternity.

Example of introductory draft exercise on a group of poems related in theme

Why so wan and pale (Suckling): *My luv is like a red, red rose* (Burns); *Shall I compare thee to a summer's day* (Shakespeare); *The Good-Morrow* (Donne); *Neutral Tones* (Hardy); *The Picnic* (John Logan)

A.   Identification of aspect

Why so wan and pale Lovesickness. Foolishness of one-sided love.

My luv is like a red, red rose Happiness of being in love. Lover able to do anything.

Shall I compare thee to a summer's day Joy in beauty of loved person. Inspiration of love.

The Good-Morrow Thrill of waking love. Lovers becoming one.

Neutral Tones Story of married love fading.

The Picnic First love. Completely new understanding.

B.   Ways in which poems open into one another

All poems show the powerful effect of love.

Wonder and happiness:

My luv is like the melodie
That's softly played in tune

> (*My luv is like a red, red rose*)

Shall I compare thee to a summer's day
Thou art more lovely and more temperate

> (*Shall I compare thee to a summer's day*)

And now good-morrow to our waking souls

> (*The Good-Morrow*)

It was then some bright thing came in my eyes . . .

> (*The Picnic*)

Love gives new power. The lover can do anything:

Love till the end of the world:
> Till all the seas gang dry, my Dear,
> And the rocks melt wi' the sun

>> (*My luv is like a red, red rose*)

Make a poem in which beauty lives for ever:

> But thy eternal summer shall not fade . . .
> When in eternal lines to time thou grow'st

>> (*Shall I compare thee to a summer's day*)

Shut out the rest of the world:

> For love, all love of other sights controules
> And makes one little room, an everywhere

>> (*The Good-Morrow*)

Become one with the person loved:

> Let us possesse one world, each hath one, and is one.

>> (*The Good-Morrow*)

In my hand join the sound and word in hers
As in one name said, or in one cupped hand.

> (*The Picnic*)

Effect of love not returned: *Why so pale and wan*
> Foolishness and helpnessness. Lover unable to think of anything else. Silly with love, pale and speechless.

Effect of love that has died: *Neutral Tones*
> Whole world affected. Everything grey and cold. Lover unable to forget the misery and bitterness of *that winter day* when love died although it happened *years ago*.

Thinking points and the individual draft record

To keep a written record of oral collaboration is to construct a personal reference book to a poetry course. The work gives practice in the move from speech to writing, fixes experience more surely in memory, causes the reader to look and think again, makes room for new recognitions. To support them in making a draft record of the way they possess a poem, pupils are given a set of thinking points. These are not general but matched to the particular poem. They invite the reader to re-enter the poem, remind him of what he knows, provide him with a framework and items of vocabulary, prompt him to discover both what he understands and what he does not understand, tempt him to go 'beyond the information given'. A set of thinking points is a form of individual tuition. How much is demanded depends on what given pupils are capable of doing; thinking points are matched to the ability of the class as well as to the poem. Generally, a set guides the pupil to deal with a number of aspects, but it may of course be limited in range, particularly for weaker pupils. How pupils use the help varies. Those who are in difficulties once they take up a pen find it easier to follow the same order as that in the set and to use the points as headings. Quicker pupils are encouraged to use the support more freely and not to feel constrained to follow the order exactly. Every pupil does not have to make a record for every poem — certainly not if an open course is being followed. Thinking points are made available for all poems, and pupils make their own selection of those they want to record. A final point: pupils are encouraged to record difficulties as well as clarities, not to be afraid of acknowledging uncertainties and dissatisfactions, to ask questions as well as to answer them.

Some examples

The Companion (Y. Yevtushenko)
A childhood memory dislodged, brought into the air. Identify the memory. Think of the poet as watching a scrap of film. Notice the details that he hears and sees clearly and those that are vague. What

thoughts are outside the film, belong to the present? What gives the reader who has never had a similar experience a hold on the poem?

Travelling through the Dark (William Stafford)
Get incident and setting clear in your imagination. Notice what catches your attention as you read. *I thought hard for all of us*: What have *we* to do with the event? Think about the title, the two kinds of swerving, what makes the writer hesitate, the car *aimed ahead*, the listening *wilderness*. What does the writer's thinking *hard* make you think?

Futility (Wilfred Owen)
Only two stanzas, each a different way of thinking and feeling. What gives each its different tone? How are the two locked together in image as well as shape? Think about the distance travelled from first line to last. Select a word you find particularly rich and examine how it works in the poem as a whole.

Ozymandias (Shelley)
First thoughts:
the image of the poem that sticks in your mind; the lesson the poem teaches; the feeling that comes across.
Second thoughts:
Two ways of understanding the inscription? Take the rest of the poem bit by bit. When does meaning stay fixed? When, besides the inscription, does a word or a line carry two possible meanings? Examine what Shelley does with the sonnet form. Connect this with the ambiguity of meaning.

Extract from *The Prelude Book 1* (The stealing of the boat) Wordsworth
Two worlds—one immediately visible, the other becoming visible. Find the immediately visible world first, locating where you share most easily in what the boy sees and does. Where does the second world emerge? What most terrifies the boy about it? How does the experience affect his relationship with the first world? Can you share the strange experience? If so, what phrases from the poem move through your mind? If not, where do you lose touch with what is going on? Suggest a title for the extract.

Love (Herbert)
Who is *Love*? What experience is Herbert trying to find words for? Is his approach head-on or sideways? How is your understanding affected by the emphasis on looking, by the fact that the word *Love* is never replaced by *he*, by the change to direct speech after the first stanza? What feeling does the poem leave you with? Where do you see the dialogue as taking place? Does the poem puzzle you at all?

The Whitsun Weddings (Philip Larkin)
Follow the journey of the poet's mind. Think about what part of his mind the reader is in touch with first; where this changes and what signals the change; how the poet's reaction to the wedding-groups advances from seeing the members to thinking about what is going on in their minds; the difference of the way he thinks about the couples who join the train. At the end how deep does his thinking search? Any surprise in the simile of the *arrow-shower* in the last two lines? How do you understand it? Notice the stanza shape: how does it match both the journey of the train and the journey of thinking? Why the short second line and the way the stanzas are connected? What is your overall reaction to this poem?

To his Coy Mistress (Marvell)
What can you say about this poem? To start with, can you say what it is about? Test the following suggestions: argument to persuade a hesitating lover or reflection on love and time; surge of desire or explosion of impatience; joy of love or torment of love; shortness of life or length of love; possibility or impossibility of defeating time; ironic or reverent view of love . . . How the poem is made. Notice the behaviour of the first two lines—large ideas against practical frustration. Follow the expansion/contraction throughout—extravagance against plainness, distance against nearness, ages against moment, mind against body, solemnity against play, and so on.
The poem falls into three parts: Suggest an identifying heading for each.
Explore the activity of the metaphors in the lines *But at my back . . .vast eternity*, and in the lines *Let us roll . . . iron gates of life*.
How is the *ball* metaphor a metaphor for the poem the reader has as well as for the poet's experience?
Effect of sure rhyming throughout the poem—given the passion of feeling? Where does rhyme convey that the poet has to strive hard to master his feeling?
What do you still want to say? What can you not say?

Handling an 'unseen' poem

Every class showing of a poem prepares pupils for handling an 'unseen'; the habit of the draft record provides them with a method for doing so in exam conditions. They know that the draft work is not rough work scribbled on the back page, but an important stage in the exercise to be taken thoughtfully and presented clearly; evidence which is of interest to their audience—teacher or examiner—as well as to themselves. They learn to use instructions on an exam paper as they use thinking points for making a record of oral collaboration.

Exercises in private collaboration can start as soon as the children have heard enough poetry to be able to use the inner ear when they read a poem silently. The kind of written response looked for keeps pace with increasing knowledge of how much there is to say. In junior years it is simply a matter of what private reading makes them want to say, recording impressions as in the *I sing of a maiden* example. Other suggestions occur in chapter 2. Later, a fuller exploration is looked for.

For slow pupils or pupils who lack confidence, poems chosen for this purpose will be well within reach, poems whose meaning is likely to be grasped at once. But with classes confident of their ability to tackle the unknown, choice should not be confined to the obvious. Much can, and should, be dared in the safety of the classroom. It is an opportunity for keeping alive the fact that the reader does not have to understand everything about a poem to have something valuable to say about it – even a poem on an exam paper. Indeed, a practical consequence of some mountain-climbing in the classroom is that the exam poem loses its alarm.

The approach is again the approach of the draft record. Thinking points are provided to help the reader to find his way on his own; they are designed to make up for the missing intersubjectivity of class collaboration. Variety in the instructions accustoms pupils to different ways of approaching an 'unseen'.

The Owl (Edward Thomas)

When you have read the poem two or three times, put it away and reduce the event to a note the writer might have made in his diary. Start, for instance: Long walk in the cold. Glad to reach the inn.

Now read the poem again watching how your note grows into a poem. Each stanza contains at least one contrast. Identify the contrasts. Which gives you the strongest impression of the writer's feeling? Which makes his thinking plainest for you?

Twice the poet twists the normal order of words to make a rhyme. Is a rhyme the only result of the twist?

What two senses has the word *salted* in the last stanza?

The owl's cry: How is the reader made to hear it as he reads? How does it change the direction the poem seems to be taking in the opening stanza?

The last stanza: Does it simply gather the thinking and feeling together or open a new thinking? Does it prompt any question in your mind? What is surprising about the word *rejoice* coming at the end of such a poem?

The Midnight Skaters (Edmund Blunden)

What expectations does the title raise? Read the poem once. Does it meet your expectations? Make a note of any parts where your mind slid over without understanding.

Now take hold of each stanza in turn. The scene in the first stanza: What have the hop-poles to do with the reader's sense of the depth of the pond? What is unusual about the word *steeples* as it is used here? In what sense is the word *sound* being used? Sensation of this stanza? The jump of thought in the second stanza: What happens to the image of the pond? Effect of the elaborate *Earth's heedless sons and daughters* for skaters? Of *he has his engines set* for death? Sensation of this stanza? What direction might the poem have taken in the third stanza? What direction does it in fact take? Are you surprised? What does the pond mean? What metaphor is worked out through the stanza? Sensation?

Notice that a different sentence type is used for each stanza. Identify the three types. How does each match what is going on in the stanza and set the reader both imagining and understanding?

Explore the metaphors *black bed*, *crystal parapet*, *ball-floor*.

So what is the poem about?

Auguries of Innocence (Blake)

This poem isn't easy. Don't expect to understand it fully. Take it whole to start with. Listen for the sound and tone of the speaker's voice, the rhythmic movement of the lines, without stopping to worry out a meaning. What tone, what voice? What dominant feeling comes through? Now begin to pick up the meaning. The first four lines may or may not appear to make sense to you. Leave them and give your attention to the auguries in the first part—up to *Beats all the lies you can invent*. (Auguries means signs or predictions.) What warning or message is being repeated through the series of examples? Leave the parts you find obscure and go on to the second part. Think out the view of human life expressed in the lines *It is right it should be so . . .* to *Runs a joy with silken twine*. Use your understanding of these lines to guide you through the rest of the poem. Think of the poet as trying to make sense of the joy and woe of the world. Again, don't get stuck on what you find obscure. What parts give you the most satisfaction, make you want to applaud? What kind of man is the speaker? What does he value, what does he condemn? Can you make anything of the last four lines? Go back to the first four lines. What do you make of them now? Come out of the poem. Does it leave you with a sense of hope or of despair? The poem was written nearly two centuries ago. Has it lost its punch?

   The above is intended for pupils of some maturity and energy. For less mature pupils only a shortened version is manageable as an 'unseen', omitting, for example, lines 19–28, 35–38, 45–50, 67–72, 81–84, 91–106, 113–118, 125–128. Thinking points are simplified accordingly. Readers are again told not to expect to understand everything. It helps to include the suggestion that at the heart of the poet's view of the world is his belief that every part of it, however small, matters to the whole.

Comparing 'unseen' poems

Pupils need to have plenty of experience of comparing poems as a communal activity before they are set the exercise as an 'unseen'. The work demands a discrimination which can come only with experience, the ability, for instance, not to be distracted by superficial similarities and dissimilarities; the ability not to let preference for one poem prevent listening to the other; the ability to keep the two in view together rather than explore each separately.

Again, oral collaboration is the starting-ground for independent written work. Making a record of oral comparison is a way of introducing the exercise. A way of taking it a stage further is to work out with the pupils a set of thinking points, based on what they have learned from various communal explorations. What is evolved will not be applicable to every poem; writers will need to select these points which are worth using with a given pair of poems.

Poems compared as a class exercise:

A. *To my Mother* (George Barker); *In Memory of my Mother* (Patrick Kavanagh).
B. *And death shall have no dominion* (Dylan Thomas); *Death, be not proud* (Donne).
C. *The Unknown Citizen* (Auden); *Prayer before Birth* (MacNeice).
D. *Landscape with the Fall of Icarus* (William Carlos Williams); *Musée des Beaux Arts* (Auden).
E. *Spring* (Hopkins); *In Just Spring* (e.e. cummings).
F. *Felix Randall* (Hopkins); *A Peasant* (R.S. Thomas).

Thinking points evolved:

First impressions
Take up a position between the two voices. Give each a hearing. Is a connection immediately obvious? Notice points of contact recognized at once.
If a connection is not immediately obvious, identify what each poet seems to be talking about. Does this suggest a connection? (C).

Poet and subject
What specific aspect of the subject are the poets attending to? Does this make the connection clearer? Notice overlapping and separation. (All pairs.)
What happens to the starting subject? Does the poet's attention in both poems remain fixed (A, B, C) or travel elsewhere in one or in both poems (D, E, F).
How strongly are the poet's emotions involved? To the same degree in both poems, similar or dissimilar emotions? (All pairs).

Method of making
Form: No surprise in shape of the poem on the page in both (A, B, C, F). Unusual in one or in both (D, E).
Language: Close to normal patterns or trying out new patterns. Rich in image or sparing. Sense of ease or effort. (All pairs.)
Rhythm: Singing or talking or thinking. Racing or advancing steadily or moving unpredictably. (All pairs).

Poem and Reader (All pairs).
First impression strengthened or changed. Drawn into poem or remaining outside. Sense of having learned something or seeing something more clearly. Left with a question or an answer.
Attracted by one more than by the other. Want to keep both or neither.

Writing up a draft record

It is best, I think, to leave the task of writing up a draft record until several poems have been dealt with in draft form and pupils' notebooks show that the skill has been mastered.

The move from draft record to discursive account is broken into three stages. Each stage is worked as a separate assignment and is assessed and discussed before going on to the next. A useful practice is to require pupils to hand in their original draft record with each new assignment. The practice emphasizes the importance of the draft and makes the process of transformation clear to teacher and pupil.

The first stage is selection of shape. Pupils are shown how to do this by the method described in *The biography of a poem* (see chapter 4). It is made clear that there are a number of possibilities to choose from. (It is wise to spell these out clearly for less able pupils.) Each pupil then chooses a poem for which he has already made a draft record, rereads both poem and record, and decides on the order of a written-up account. This is not a matter simply of general headings such as meaning, craft, reader's response, but is a draft outline of the ideas which will be dealt with in each section. See *The biography of a poem* for examples.

The second stage is expanding the outline arrived at by selecting appropriate items from the original draft record which will illustrate the points made. Note form is still used. For example, Section A of a pupil's draft outline for *Earthy Anecdote* (Wallace Stevens) read:

First impression—scene of energetic action on a wide plain, very vivid, immediately clear to the reader. This was then expanded:

First impression: Scene of energetic action on a plain in Oklahoma—a herd of bucks clattering stopped by a firecat *bristling in the way*. Exact movement of bucks *clattering* and *swerving* and of firecat leaping *to the right, to the left* described so that reader sees the scene immediately.

The third stage is the actual writing up. The point to stress for the pupils is that they now have not only ideas organized in a certain way but most of the vocabulary they need to write up their ideas coherently. With less able pupils it is helpful to confine the first attempt at writing up to one section only of what is arrived at in the second stage. This gives them time to concentrate on the job of turning notes into sentences. All classes, in first attempts at the assignment, are instructed to stick to the decisions made in the first and second stages. For later attempts there is no such restriction; pupils are encouraged to include the new ideas inspired by the reconsideration writing up involves.

6

'The ancient dialogue between man and his world'

(Wallace Fowlie)

Readers whose school experience of poetry has been a source of active enjoyment are, by the time they embark on senior work, readers who have already acquired what Jonathan Culler calls 'literary competence' (**32**). They do not read a poem in quite the same way as they read other matter; they bring to the act 'an implicit understanding of the operations of literary discourse which tells one what to look for' (**32**). In senior work, that competence is developed through extending both the range of poetry studied and the kind of knowledge brought to the reading of a poem. Senior students are ready for new ideas. As Helen Gardner puts it: 'If the first response to a work of art is wonder, the child of wonder is curiosity. The satisfaction of curiosity, which is a great pleasure, brings a renewal of the sense of words and so leads to new curiosity' (**14**). So students are introduced to new ideas: ideas about the wider context of period and genre; ideas about continuity; about the power of high poetic achievement to keep its freshness across centuries as well as ideas about what today's poet is contributing to the life of language; ideas about the nature and value of the poetic experience as well as the ideas prompted by particular poems.

'A civilization is judged by its amateurs' (**33**). The competence is the competence of amateurs, not the competence of the professional critic. We can introduce students to critical ideas, traditional and contemporary, as long as the ideas are ideas they can use themselves in their reading. What we do not want is that they should, in anxiety about an exam, pick up the habit of pretending to a competence they simply can't have. We do not want them, for instance, to produce essays in literary history which refer blandly to works they have not actually read. It is worth introducing them to some critical work after, not before, they have explored a poet's work themselves. The important thing is that when a literary critic enters the classroom dialogue, he does so as a reader who has something new to show, not as a rival to the poet and not as a model of expression. His value is that personal enjoyment and understanding are increased by what he has to say. If his presence does not send readers back to the poet and his poetry, he has no place in the enterprise. Again, when students choose to use his insights in their own draft records or essays, they must acknowledge the source; they should not offer his arguments as if they were their own.

Sampling a poetry course

Whatever kind of course, prescribed or open, students are following, the starting-point is still the competence they already have, the capacity to attend 'without any irritable reaching after fact and reason'. An approach that I have found to work well is to give sustained attention during the first year to the drama and novel sections of a course and to give only odd periods to sampling the poetry section. New work is visited rather than studied—as one might go to an art gallery to see for the first time masterpieces known only through hearsay or in reproduction. There is a deliberate pause in the 'studying' of poetry. The visiting is not attended by specific tasks. Students may choose to keep a record of visits, but they are not required to do so. The intention is to lessen the pressure that working for an exam inevitably causes, to let the experience be an experience of art rather than a stiffening of intellectual muscles. Such periods are a pause for refreshment, an initial satisfaction of curiosity about poets who are household names. Readers have space to make contact with the poetry in their time before attempting to see it in its own time. Since they know that this is only a sampling, and that exam requirements will be dealt with later, they can relax their attention. When formal study begins, there is already a point of pleasure to start from.

Poetry seminars

Another form of refreshment is talking about aspects of the poetic enterprise, seminars in which the students examine their previous and current experience; take up and shake out ideas about the continuing 'ancient dialogue between man and his world in which the word is the very special gift and privilege of man, the talisman which awakens a hidden network of correspondences' (**34**). Seminar discussion should, I think, be a feature of poetry work right through the senior years. It is a necessary counter to the problem of any exam course: the problem of works of art appearing as objects to be wrapped up at school and then set aside, as objects whose mystery is an illusion to be dispelled rather than an irreducible fact. The topic of a seminar will frequently be the intersubjective showing of a poem, but there should also be occasions in which ideas about poetry are explored. There is a wide range of topics to choose from (**35**) and this is an area where teacher and students are free from the constraints of prescription. In the process various questions are raised which serve as a background for formal study. Different teachers will be interested in different topics and it is the topic which interests the teacher that is most likely to fire the interest of the students. Poets themselves should be a frequent source. What poets have to say about their craft is a healthy balance to the amount that readers have to say, be they teachers, students or critics. There is plenty of material, ranging across the centuries, to draw from. Seminar topics are given to the students some time beforehand so that they can prepare for discussion. Preparation means thinking of the topic in relation to their experience of actual poems; one mark of a successful seminar is the range of poetry referred to in discussion of the starting idea.

Some examples
'Poetry is above all a way of using words to say things which could not possibly be said in any other way'. C. Day Lewis (**36**). A poem 'is what should be said'. Ivor Winters (**37**)
Poetry 'should strike the reader as a wording of his own highest thoughts, and appear almost Remembrance.' Keats. (**13**) 'Poetry is the language in which man explores his own amazement' Christopher Fry (**36**).
'Poetry is a response to the daily necessity of getting the world right'. Wallace Stevens (**38**)
'In the fearful years of the Yezhov terror I spent seventeen months in prison queues in Leningrad. One day somebody 'identified' me. . . . She suddenly came out of that trance so common to us all and whispered in my ear. . . . 'Can you describe this?' And I said: 'Yes, I can.' . . . And then something like a shadow of a smile crossed what had once been her face' Anna Akhmatova (**39**).
'The poet as artist is, by the common nature of his medium, the poet as citizen' Josephine Miles (**40**). Artists 'remind the Management of something managers need to be reminded of, namely that the managed are people with faces, not anonymous members, that *Homo Laborans* is also *Homo Ludens*' Auden (**38**).
'It is when words sing that they give that absolute moving attention which is beyond their prose powers'. R.P. Blackmur (**35**) 'Can prose become poetry through typographical arrangement? I rather think it can'. Edwin Morgan (**35**).
Examine *Perfect* (Hugh MacDiarmid) and its source in *The Blue Bed* (Glyn Jones) (**35**).
'*The fascination of what's difficult*' Yeats. Identify different causes of difficulty. Does the difficulty 'dry up the sap' of the reader's pleasure? What is a metaphor? Take a number of metaphors (selected by students). How many can be turned into similes?
Blank verse in different voices. Use a passage from each of three masters of the form: Shakespeare, Milton, Wordsworth. Investigate variations on the iambic pentameter line, coincidence of line-ending and normal syntactic break, use of sound patterns other than metre. Try reading each passage as if it were prose. Compare results.
Pope and the rhyming couplet: Take a passage at random from *The Rape of the Lock*. Investigate the connections the rhyming persuades the

reader to make: rhymes which bring together incompatible words, rhymes which cause a quick puncture, rhymes which start a slow puncture. Relate observations to the sense of a smooth surface which may at any moment split open and reveal a chasm.

Read a critic's analysis of a poem the students have not found difficult. For example, Winifred Nowottny on Shakespeare's *That time of year* (**8**), William Empson on Marvell's *The Garden* (**41**), C.M. Bowra on Keats's *Ode on a Grecian Urn* (**42**), W.K. Wimsatt on Blake's *London* (**18**). How does the analysis affect the readers' relationship with the poem?

Voice and vision

Senior work normally offers students the experience of reading a relatively long poem or a number of poems by the same writer. For the majority the experience is new in that it involves listening to a single voice speaking at length rather than the many changing voices they are accustomed to. The first impact is cumulative, made over a period of time instead of in a few minutes. What matters in the first encounter is tuning in to the single voice, letting the poetry disclose the lineaments of the new music. The emphasis of introductory remarks is on the act of listening, the concentration of the ear. With some work it is necessary to provide certain points of contact; at this stage, these are confined to information without which the music would be an incomprehensible blur. Thus, before reading Dryden's *MacFlecknoe*, students would need some basic facts about the real life source of the satire. Before reading *Paradise Lost* it would be wise to make sure they have some precise ideas about 'man's first disobedience' and the fall of the angels. But it would not be necessary at this stage to discuss epic form. Nor would it be necessary to preface a selection of Wordsworth with a discourse on Romanticism. The trouble is that such a preamble is likely to get in the way of hearing the voice. It is still worth giving the innocent ear freedom to make its own discoveries without benefit of received opinion. Say, for instance, that the material is a selection of metaphysical poetry. What signs of a 'school' do unprejudiced readers perceive? Do they recognize a common attitude to what a poem should say and how it should say it, to subject, to length, to stanza shape, to image and idiom? Are they aware that the poets are living in the same world? In my experience, the main characteristics are discovered and discovered with some of the quick interest of the metaphysical poets themselves.

Whether it is a long poem or a group of poems, the first reading can usually follow the habit of any reader who takes up a book of poems: namely to read it through, sometimes pausing to reread, and sometimes sliding across a page. What is valuable now is the students' intuitions of what is happening; it is their response which determines the amount of intervention needed. The amount of intervention varies according to the length and difficulty of the work. Obviously, more is needed with Milton than with Pope, more with Eliot than with Wordsworth. For instance, a major difficulty of *Paradise Lost* is the density of Milton's analogies, particularly when these come in massive sequence in the roll call of the angels in Book 1. Nothing would be gained by glossing each as it occurs. Much is gained if the readers are persuaded to let sound and image swarm in to fill imagination with huge shadows. Indeed, one might say that the less precise one's knowledge about individual members of the 'promiscuous crowd', the vaster the number appears.

Studying a long poem: *Paradise Lost*, Book 1

There is not, I think, any predetermined shape for studying a long poem. Different poems have a way of suggesting their own logic of attention. The order in which different aspects are taken up is perhaps best guided by the curiosity of the readers. Aspects open into one another, raise new questions, require new knowledge or closer observation of different parts of the poem. External knowledge (historical, linguistic, biographical) is introduced as it is needed, not separately but arising from attention to the poem itself.

A starting-point emerges in the unstructured comment that follows the first reading. With *Paradise Lost* Book 1 this is most frequently the figure of Satan; closer study might thus begin with observation of his 'character'. Examine what Satan's speeches reveal of the immense inner war: the greatness and the signs of ruinous smallness; the power to be first and the disabling self-deceiving vanity; the courage to endure and the resentful doubt of success; the defiant choice of evil and the despair at what has been lost; the confessed pain and what Coleridge calls 'the alcohol of egotism'. Students readily connect the self-revelation of the speeches with the way a Shakespearean character reveals himself. This makes relevant the information that Milton had earlier thought of writing a play on the theme rather than a poem, which suggests examining other dramatic elements.

For instance, how the war within Satan finds a way to action and reaction outside him. The dialogue with Beelzebub has elements of theatre. But the binding of the legions to his will—could Milton have achieved that in play-form? This brings readers closer to Milton's dramatic vision: the sense of his being an interpreting eye-witness to a drama too large to be contained in a conventional theatre. Observe how Satan is made present, and the delay in seeing him as against hearing him. On what stage is the voice heard? How do stage and voice prepare imagination to accept the superhuman figure that gradually becomes visible? Examine what Milton does as he prepares to move from narrative to dialogue; the double point of view at once confirming

Satan's self-image and subverting it. Clear examples are lines 238–241, 619–621. Does this double view cause difficulty for a modern reader? The question prompts thinking about the different competence of a seventeenth-century reader and the need for a modern reader to remember the theological beliefs and attitudes of Milton's day. This would be a point at which to introduce information about Milton's own religious commitment.

From this, perhaps, to the moral vision informing the conception of Satan. What for Milton is the prime sin which distorts seeming virtue? How does Book 1 show great virtue already advanced in decay? Portrait of an archangel ruined or of a man creating his own destruction? Ancient moral myth or perennial moral reality? This opens the question of the politics of Hell and the notion of Satan as absolute ruler, which leads to information about Milton's political history and discussion of the ambivalence in the image of the council at the end of the book.

From Satan to Satan's kingdom. Knowledge of Milton's cosmography is not essential to understanding Book 1 and is hardly worth dealing with, except perhaps briefly in connection with the hurling from Heaven and the rumour of Earth's creation. What is important is the physical and psychological image of Hell. Readers have no difficulty sharing in this. What do they make of Eliot's criticism that 'at no period is the visual imagination conspicuous in Milton's poetry' (**43**)? What response do they find themselves making to the vision of Hell, a terror for the imagination which reason rejects? Consider the effect on the reader of Satan's claim that the mind can make a heaven of hell.

By this point much of the book will have been reread. Now the students are set to read it through privately, rediscovering the narrative line and watching the mastery of the telling: the alternation of description, dialogue, action; the way the reader is released from the infernal regions and given a point of reference in the seas, mountains, skies, even the homes of earth. Something of the range of imaginative variety is caught if, for instance, the early description of Hell in lines 50–69 is set against the gathering of the host in Pandemonium in lines 757–798.

The reading through opens the question of Milton's private frame of reference; the massive world of his learning and his memory of places seen before he became blind. Students cannot be expected to acquire the knowledge of a reader educated in the classics. What they can do is to make a virtue of ignorance and yield to the strangeness. They do not need to be able to explain the allusions in order to participate imaginatively in their effect. The point is that Milton does not simply list names; the names are embedded in sensuous action which any reader can experience.

Another question the rereading leads to is that of Milton's intention; the moral purpose, the warning and the challenge to the reader enacted in the opening lines. The high purpose makes a surer impact now that the readers have experienced the fulfilment. The impact is strengthened by information about the circumstances of composition; the isolation that followed the end of the Commonwealth and in particular the extraordinary fact of the twenty years of poetic silence that preceded the writing. (Few students will be equipped to wonder at the difference between the early work and *Paradise Lost*, though occasionally curiosity is keen enough to send some of them to look at the early poems.) The invocation of the Muse of Greek poetry as well as of the Holy Spirit raises the question of Milton's deliberate choice of the epic form. By now the students have firsthand experience of epic poetry, which is ground for some information about the history of the form and discussion of what Milton does with it.

By now too the language has had time to work its effect and become to some extent familiar music. Nowadays few students are equipped to recognize the connections between Milton's diction and Latin, but this does not prevent their perceiving the distinctive abnormality of the handling of language. A description of the main features of vocabulary and syntax and an understanding of the gain in relation to purpose are well within their competence. In the light of the experience of the poem, what do they think of Keats's comment that *Paradise Lost* 'is a corruption of our language' (**13**) and Eliot's view in the first Milton essay that he may be 'considered as having done damage to the English language' (**43**)? It is also worth giving some attention to Milton's handling of language in the context of other poets: earlier poets whose work he knew and those writing at the same time. The influence of Spenser is not a profitable question since students rarely know Spenser. But they are familiar with Shakespeare, and usually have some experience of Donne and Marvell. A manageable and clear demonstration for students of Milton's independence of the tradition being established in his own time is Dryden. Take a passage from *Absolom and Achitophel* or from *Mac Flecknoe* and compare the exact and buoyant geometry of Dryden's harmony with the daring intricacy of Milton's.

At last, perhaps, stand back from the adventure of the reading: where have the readers been—among men or gods?

Reading a poet: T.S. Eliot *Selected Poems*

Time has not much lessened the peculiar difficulty of Eliot for new readers. His work is a high challenge to their literary competence. It is also an immensely stimulating one. Not the least reward of taking up the challenge is a deeper understanding of the continuing mystery of the poetic 'raid on the inarticulate'. To read Eliot is to share in his sense of the impossibility of exhausting the meaning of a poem (**43**) and to find difficulty not an obstacle to be got out of the way but part of the enjoyment.

The relatively small size of the output is an advantage in classroom study. The *Selected Poems* represent a sizeable amount of the full œuvre, proportionately much larger than can be offered from other major poets. There is enough material for firsthand experience of the development of voice and vision. The date of Eliot's entry into literary history means that most readers already have direct knowledge of what preceded and what followed that date, providing them with a context they do not always have for other shifts in tradition. The innovativeness is vigorous enough for students to feel the shock of the new as the first readers did. They can feel 'on the pulse' the 'ancient dialogue' in the act of being renewed, and respond, in spite of difficulty, to an accent and idiom that comes 'almost like a Remembrance'.

The method of reading through the poems with a minimum of discussion does not work with Eliot, unless the students are exceptionally precocious. It causes too much frustration. It is better to take the poems in groups, making the stages of the 'raid on the inarticulate' the focus, and giving time for the poems themselves to refine the readers' competence.

The main difficulty is the allusiveness of Eliot's technique. Students come to terms easily enough with the unexpected transitions, the leaps and twists of music and image, but not with the wide range of learned allusion. The activity of the allusions in the texture and meaning is an aspect to introduce gradually; the problem is better not tackled until it is a key cause of incomprehension. For instance, the allusions are not a major obstacle in *Prufrock and Other Observations*. Students normally recognize and accept without alarm a number of them, and I should not, at this stage, press information on them about those they miss. The allusiveness of *Gerontion* is another matter. The poem is sufficiently dramatic to have a profound effect on readers who are unaware of the allusive density. It causes the kind of wonder that leads to curiosity, and satisfaction of the curiosity can deepen the wonder. This does not mean that every allusion must be exposed and categorized and committed to memory. If intuition has grasped the effect without recognizing the source, I should leave well enough alone. This happens with the adaptation from Middleton, *I that was near your heart* . . . . But the cluster of allusions round the figure of Christ does need to be explicated, in order to grasp the question at the heart of the poem. Readers cannot join in the game of ideas in the Quatrain poems without knowing the allusions and now this feature of the manner is deliberately hunted home. One result of explicit attention at this point is that the readers are less bothered by the several 'fragments' of *The Waste Land*; they are accustomed to the challenge. Again, as in *Gerontion*, the allusions are often so dramatically or lyrically assimilated into the new fabric that they communicate before they are understood.

Eliot is one of the great melodists of English verse and for a true enjoyment of his poetry the reader's own auditory imagination needs to be always active. A study of the virtuosity of his prosodic discoveries is not possible in the classroom. What is possible is a constant listening; recordings of the poet's own reading should form part of the experience. Frequent submission to the sound of the verse goes a long way to correcting the imbalance caused by grappling with problems of comprehension.

'Explanation,' says Eliot, 'may be a necessary preparation for understanding a poem. But to understand a poem it is also necessary, and I should say in most instances still more necessary, that we should endeavour to grasp what the poetry is aiming to be . . . .' (**38**). The comment suggests a principle of approach. Sometimes it is necessary to preface a poem with explanation of a kind which does not provide a prose paraphrase but does provide a way of listening. It is necessary with the Quatrain poems and *The Waste Land*, for instance. But sometimes it is more effective 'to spring the poem on them' as Eliot says in another context (**43**). This is worth trying with the *Prufrock* poems. Instead of starting at the shallow end with *Preludes* and *Rhapsody on a Windy Night*, throw the readers in at the deep end with *Prufrock*. The advantage is twofold. In the first place there is the exhilarating shock of the new – a chance of the same excitement that 1915 readers of the poem felt. In the second place, when readers realize that they can, however clumsily they move, save themselves from drowning, they face the open sea of the later poems with confidence and a sense of adventure. Throughout the study the 'endeavour to grasp what the poem is aiming to be' is of prime importance. Eliot demands from the reader the acceptance that he has 'not made this show purposelessly' and the willingness to work at discovering the purpose, the intent of each new 'raid'.

Some suggestions for studying the *Selected Poems*

Preliminary: Recall the students' knowledge of Victorian and Georgian poetry. What readers were accustomed to finding when they opened a book of poems: the look of the page, the sound of the verse, the subject matter. Remind them that Hopkins had not yet been published.

Prufrock and *Portrait of a Lady*
Read *Prufrock* without preliminary comment, like 1915 readers, including a translation of the Dante epigraph (a necessary stage-direction) as part of what the listeners hear. Give initial reactions free rein. These are usually as mixed as those of the first readers, ranging from excited pleasure through incomprehension to outrage. Turn to the *Portrait*.

Advise the students to let themselves go with the tide, to *let the scene arrange itself*. The narrative line is seldom missed even by those who have made nothing of *Prufrock*. Examine what this narrative 'is aiming to be'. What substance has the relationship, the woman who utters thoughts and wishes aloud and the man who does not open his mouth? Examine the play between the outer situation '*particularly remarked*', and what happens in the narrator's consciousness. Depths or shallows? Feelings or sensations? Accuse the narrator as he accuses himself. Of what? How often does the reader see his own face in the glass, hear the *dull tom-tom* in his own brain, feel his *self-possession gutter*?

Turn to *Prufrock* again. Start perhaps from where discussion of the *Portrait* ended, with the reader's meeting himself in the poem. The *Portrait* aimed to be a new way of exploiting narrative; *Prufrock* aims to be a new kind of dramatic monologue. Compared with the *Portrait*, how much of the external situation (the tea-party) actually influences the flickering of thought and feeling? Pick up from the *Portrait* the phrase *my buried life* as a clue to what is happening in *Prufrock*. Pick up points of reference within *Prufrock*, for instance, *the muttering retreats* and *In short, I was afraid*. Try reading the poem as a series of retreats from *the overwhelming question*. Irony of the word *overwhelming*? Is the question formulated? Is any gesture of the poem completed, brought to certainty —even the last? Irony of the title? Can the readers piece together a character, or does that too slide out of reach, *borrow every changing shape*? *It is impossible to say just what I mean*! Has the effort to do the impossible been *worthwhile*?

Gerontion and the Quatrain poems

The difficulty of *Gerontion* is not so much the allusiveness as the act of imaginative projection demanded of the reader. The reader is asked to confront a terror of meaninglessness which the poem does not resolve. Take it for what it is, not the soliloquizing of *Prufrock* but true dramatic soliloquy, intensely and narrowly concentrated. The scene does not, as in the earlier poems, 'arrange itself', but is arranged. There is a logic of development: situation and setting are localized at some length, the old man, the particulars of the *decayed house*. Present connects with past in the irruption of anguish in the first *Christ the tiger* passage—the darkness of unattained promised meaning, a darkness confirmed by the useless unbidden memories of figures from the past. This is followed by the effort of intellect, an act of willed thinking which finds only signs of meaninglessness. In the second *Christ the tiger* passage the anguish of darkness returns and is followed by another effort of intellect, this time bidding a memory significant for the speaker, and judging past passion and present loss of passion. The mind is then whirled out of its *thousand small deliberations* (an echo of *Hamlet*?) by a vision of death. Finally, there is cessation of memory and effort in the return to the *decayed house*.

Students can make their way through the logic of the drama. Certainly they are moved by it. They can sense the irony of the last two lines, which remove the framework of logic that speaker and reader rely on. They can recognize too that there are ambiguities in the poem, but I am not sure that most can rise to enjoyment of the rhythm of ambiguity. The ambiguity of *signs are taken for wonders* is made clear in the concrete examples of profanity which follow. The ambiguities of history are patiently demonstrated in the series of paradoxes in the *Think now* passage, difficult but not ungraspable. But in the second *Christ the tiger* passage there is no making clear, no demonstration to lead the reader to sure identification of the ambiguity he senses. In the lost passion passage ambiguity is again worked out, demonstrated. But the ambiguity of the death passage whirls out of reach. One can say only that it may imply the hope that death cleanses confusion or the despair that death is the ultimate fracturing of life as meaning.

After the stretching of imagination *Gerontion* demands, the game of ideas in the Quatrain poems is a pause for recreation. There is no way round the allusion problem in these poems and I would suggest taking them as puzzles which may or may not exhilarate those who try to solve them. Divide the class into seven groups. Each group takes on the job of attempting to solve the riddle of one of the poems. They start by seeing what they can make of the poem without notes, and then examine how understanding is helped by knowing the allusions (**44**). Each group reports its findings to the class. The whole class discusses whether the poems work as satire and what has happened to the *overwhelming question*.

The Waste Land and *Ash Wednesday*
There is no shortage of exegetical commentary on *The Waste Land*. The important thing is to be moderate in the use made of it in the classroom, to leave room for the students to find their way to the meanings. Introductory comment is necessary. The title directs the reader to read with the Grail legend in mind and a knowledge of the legend and its symbolic meaning is minimum equipment. It is also wise to suggest a way of listening, to give some indication of what the poem is aiming to be. For instance, that what lies ahead is sharing in the consciousness of a poet journeying through a modern waste land, a consciousness which carries 'all the properties of his life which churn about in his head' (**45**). In this poet's mind the experience of wide reading is as active as other kinds of experience, so the readers may expect reference to this. They are advised to let image and allusion work their effect imaginatively.

Whether the poem is first read straight through without further comment is a matter of choice for the individual teacher. My own preference is to take it in sections and to leave an uninterrupted hearing until later. The relevance of the title to each section is explained before the section is read. It also helps to suggest a focus of attention for each section. For example: The Burial of the Dead—*I will show you fear in a handful of dust*; A Game of Chess—*Are you alive or not? Is there nothing in your head?*; The Fire Sermon—View of sexual love; Death by Water —the title is sufficient; What the Thunder Said—final stage, a journey through the mountains to what end?

A cohering element in the texture is the handling of echo. Alertness to this holds the reading together and causes recognition of the 'transformation scene' strategy employed. The city of the first and third sections, which finally collapses in the last; the recurring fragments from *The Tempest*, the recurring bells, the recurring meaningless bird calls; the restless merging figures, the women, the merchants, the *hooded hordes*; the scraps of remembered journeys in the first section becoming the intent journey of the last section, and so on.

After this section-by-section reading, the poem is listened to at a sitting. The class might then break into five groups, each group being responsible for closer reading of one section. Grail allusions and allusions which are part of the readers' experience—such as the borrowings from *The Tempest*—are taken into account, but readers are not required to hunt down all allusions. The emphasis is rather on attempting to articulate what a section means for the members of the group, what they accept or reject in the vision, what they find moving, what they observe about the poet's strategies. They might also give some attention to the process of composition revealed by the orignal drafts (**46**), or this might make a seminar topic later. Findings are shared with the whole class.

The difficulty of *Ash Wednesday* is that it attempts to express that most inexpressible experience, the moment of grace, a moment which is by its nature unique to the man who experiences it. If readers are not moved by listening to the poem, no amount of explication will change matters. The yielding to grace is experienced *between word and word* or it is not experienced at all.

The poem communicates first through the beautiful manipulation of harmony, and I should invite students simply to listen, trying to relax attention of any faculty save that of hearing. After that, a way of approaching deeper understanding is to read the poem as redemption of the personal anguish of *The Waste Land*. Some examples: the city of *The Waste Land* gives way to the luminous non-places which have a private form in the imagination of each of us; the vociferous desert of a wrecked world becomes a place with *the blessing of sand*. The restless self-absorbed crowds undone by death give place to the communion of saints, the scattered singing bones and the figure of the Lady. The familiar features of the earlier manner are transfigured rather than dispensed with, so that the language of the poem is itself a metaphor for the redeemed time. The self-questioning and the uncertainty are here *proffered to oblivion*, in a humility which is *devoted, concentrated in purpose*. In *The Waste Land*, Dante was drawn on to confirm the condition of pain; here he is drawn on to confirm the hope, in the Beatrice figure and the figure of the three stairs of penance.

Choruses from *The Rock*
I cannot understand Eliot's choosing to include these pieces in the *Selected Poems*. Perhaps it is an act of self-mockery, showing how flat a serious poet can fall. I find them 'windy suspiration of forced breath', repetitious, overexplicit, musically dull, conventional in idea, dated in idiom, fatally easy to imitate. I can see no other use for this work in the classroom except as an illustration of Eliot's failing to meet his own condition that the poet should 'turn his interests into poetry, not merely meditate upon them poetically'(**43**).

Unwriting a poem

'The American linguist Edward Sapir compares language to an electric dynamo able to power a lift, but normally used simply to operate a doorbell' (**27**). Unwriting a poem is a way of increasing respect for the resources of language by investigating how poets use it to 'power a lift'. As Winifred Nowottny puts it: 'If poetry is language at full stretch, the stretching must help us to see more clearly the nature of the fabric stretched' (**8**).

The main emphasis of the exercise is linguistic, but this does not mean that it is necessary to use the models or the metalanguage of the linguistic analyst. The terms students are already familiar with are quite adequate. Some new terms may be introduced according to their usefulness. The term 'foregrounding', for instance, has the merit of being self- explanatory as well as convenient (**47**).

The unwriting shows up the distinctiveness of a poem and gives precise meaning to the handful of words commonly used to describe style, for instance simple, natural, solemn, elaborate, and so on. Readers are drawn into sharing the creative act through sharing in some of the processes of the poet's making language serve his purpose. The goal is not to come up with a definitive meaning but to make contact with the complex of meaning at work in the language.

Work of this kind can be done only with a short poem—a poem for which Ivor Winters claims that 'it is the only literary form in which the mature and civilized poet can at all times employ the best poetry of which he is capable on subject matter of major importance' (**48**). A poem is chosen for the wonder it causes in teacher or student.

An initial experiment is to unwrite a very short poem. For example, Pound's *Fan-piece, for Her Imperial Lord,*

> O fan of white silk,
>   Clear as frost on the grass-blade,
>   You also are laid aside.

It takes the reader a second to read this. In the second, he not only
decodes the words, but recreates a narrative instant which contains a
past and a future of indefinite length as well as the present of the poem.
Essentially all readers will agree that this is a story of love found and
lost. Unwriting reveals something of how this common perception is
reached.

The title specifies a certain context of period, culture, personal
relationship. Among the specified items, there is one open item—the
word *for*. Most readers will take this at first to indicate a gift prepared
by a happy lover. The apostrophizing first line invites participation in a
moment of strong feeling. There is nothing yet to tell us that this is not
a moment of sudden joy. Nor is there anything in the second line, which
presents an exquisite image. The increased line length invites lingering
and thus protracts suspense. In the third line the true situation is
suddenly clear. The feeling now surely identified has the stronger effect
because of the suspense, just as the speaker's sadness is the keener
because of previous happiness. *Laid aside* is the obvious conveyor of the
information and feeling. However, the real explosion of the narrative
occurs in the word *also*. A workaday word which is at home in any
register becomes here the word which opens up a history of finding and
losing, of then and now. The interesting thing is that the word creates
an irregularity in the haiku form. Without it, the piece would have
conformed to the conventional 5—7—5 syllable arrangement and
would still make sense—but a sense less rich. With it, the third line is a
beautifully clear working model of Pound's dictum: 'A new cadence is a
new idea'. The 'new idea' now works back over the rest of the poem.
The 'frost' image takes on a metaphysical depth which in turn affects
the *fan of white silk* and the title.

Pound is reworking a translation of a longer Chinese poem (**49**). In
the reworking, the poignancy of the original is no longer trapped in the
quaintness of a past culture. Further, by introducing an element of
suspense he makes 'the reader himself leap up at the truth which the
poet sees' (**8**).

A slumber did my spirit seal (Wordsworth)

> A slumber did my spirit seal;
>   I had no human fears:
> She seemed a thing that could not feel
>   The touch of earthly years.

> No motion has she now, no force;
>   She neither hears nor sees;
> Rolled round in earth's diurnal course,
>   With rocks, and stones, and trees.

The poem does not appear at first reading to offer any special challenge to understanding. Wordsworth appears to be simply a man speaking to men in a common language about grief.

It is syntactically straightforward. There are only two deviations from the norm: *did seal* and *no motion has she*, both of which the reader accepts as customary in verse of an earlier period. The vocabulary is undemanding. Apart from the word *diurnal*. Wordsworth uses no items which would have caused trouble for his ordinary countryman. The word *slumber* and the metaphor in the first line belong to an idiom customary in hymns and ballads.

The verse form is unremarkable, a quatrain conventional in rhyme and metre. The dominant feature of versification is the common one of parallelism. These are frequent sound parallels, both alliterative and assonantal. These multiply in the second stanza, but no line is without its thread in the web of echoes.

The parallelism of sentence structure is remarkable. The mode is set in the first stanza by the two opening simple sentences, each coextensive with a line. The third sentence continues the mode and extends it, quite normally, by adding a relative clause, which is also simple in structure. The second stanza continues the mode, but intensifies it by the inversion in the first line and the exploitation of a normal method of contraction. The first two lines of this stanza contain, in fact, four simple sentences, two in each line. In each of these the subject is *she*, the same subject, that is, as that in the third sentence of the first stanza. This repetition of *she* foregrounds the contraction used in the last two lines of the poem so that the reader unhesitatingly supplies—one might say hears—the missing 'she is'. Thus in these lines a further simple sentence appears which this time expands to fill two lines. Another syntactic forgrounding occurs across the two stanzas in the system of negatives: *no, not, no, neither, nor*.

What such analysis shows is a movement of the simple sentence which corresponds to the curve of emotion intuitively felt by the reader. Because of the repetition of *she*, three times explicitly, twice implicitly, the reader shares in the poet's sense of a world in which *she* is the only object of attention. Because the repetition works across two stanzas, it locks past and present together. The *she* plus verb structure, occurring in both affirmative and negative form, carries both love and loss.

This accords with the reader's logical understanding of the poem. Logically, he understands the first stanza as the memory of a state of past happiness and the second as the experience of a state of present grief. Intuitively, he feels that there is something strange in the way the two states are presented—an apparent absence of expected contrast. There is no feeling of joy in the first stanza; the second ends in a climax of calm. Observation discovers the source of the intuition: the first state is so presented that it already contains the second state. Now there is nothing uncommon in the fact that memory of the past is coloured by the present. What is uncommon is the way the phenomenon is enacted in the poem; not by contrast but by similarity. In the first 'memory' stanza, the slumber sealing the spirit implies a state of non-feeling. The negatives of the second state are already present in the enactment of the first state. The word *thing* already removes the beloved to the non-feeling state of rocks, stones, trees.

Further, the paradox is enacted in the behaviour of the rhymes. One effect of the exact end-rhymes is to foreground the '*seal*' metaphor by enacting a 'sealing', a bonding of the sound of the poem across the two stanzas. Notice the alliterative and assonantal links between the different rhymes and the matching of *seal/feel* with *sees/trees* and of *fears* with *force*. If we examine the words that are rhymed, we notice that something more than a bonding of sound going on. The pairs in the 'memory' stanza bring together ideas which are in some sense uneasy partners: *seal* and *feel*; *fears* and *years*. Each pair evokes troubling contraries. But those in the 'loss' stanza have a certain coherence: *force* and *course* are bound by their abstractness; *sees* and *trees* are bound by their concreteness.

The paradox is realized in other ways too. Notice the working of the word *no*. The sound value of the word dominates the second stanza and achieves an extraordinary fusion in

> No motion has she now, no force;

The alliteration foregrounds *no . . . now . . . no*. Coming where it does, the word *now*—with its connotation of the flow of time stopped—fuses life and death in intense presentness. Significantly, *now* finds its assonantal echo only in *round* of the last lines. Moreover, in the course of the poem the *no* sound passes from words of abstract connotation into words of concrete connotation—*rolled* and *stones* in the last lines. A reverse passage takes place in the transformation of the sensory perception of *The touch of earthly years* into the mental perception of *earth's diurnal course*.

What is happening is that the apparently missing contrast is being expressed through paradox, a mode which works by fusion rather than opposition. Paradox is powerfully at work in the first line of the poem. The sentence is foregrounded by being the only one which has not a personal pronoun as subject. It refers to a time when happiness was alive, but it does so in words connoting a state of non-life. (Compare Shakespeare: *Death's second self, which seals up all in rest* in Sonnet 73). The informed reader will read the line in the light of his knowledge that there was for Wordsworth a kind of sleep in which the creative spirit is most alive. The attentive reader who does not know this can, I suggest, discover it in this poem. The point is that the structure of the poem leads him to the intuition. The alliterative foregrounding compels awareness of the tension between *spirit* and the other two words of the trio: *slumber* and *seal*. What happens is that the central paradox of spirit/life and body/death comes to light. This is echoed lightly in the word *earthly* and at full strength in the final lines. Recognizing this, the reader goes on to recognize that it is sleeping spirit which perceives the truth the poem enacts: the truth that the only kind of wholeness available to men grows from a fusion of contraries. The poem realizes part of our deepest knowledge, the knowledge of contraries, and brings us to the perception that these form a single texture, a single body, as it were.

Students are naturally curious about the identity of Lucy, and the fact that there is no sure biographical answer prompts thinking about the mysterious roots of poetic inspiration. More important is the relationship between the poem and other Wordsworth poems. Other Lucy poems show the contrasting states defined by their difference, for example, *She dwelt among the untrodden ways* and *Three years she grew in sun and shower*. The 'skating' and 'boating' extracts from *The Prelude* show Wordsworth pondering his intuition of the hidden harmony of all living things. If the students are reading *Tintern Abbey* and *Ode on Intimations* they will discover clear points of contact. Invite them to assemble from these a set of references which are a gloss on this poem, both on the creative sleep and on the harmony of the final lines.

The Snow Man   (Wallace Stevens)

One must have a mind of winter
To regard the frost and the boughs
Of the pine-trees crusted with snow;

And have been cold a long time
To behold the junipers shagged with ice,
The spruces rough in the distant glitter

Of the January sun; and not to think
Of any misery in the sound of the wind,
In the sound of a few leaves,

Which is the sound of the land
Full of the same wind
That is blowing in the same bare place

For the listener, who listens in the snow,
And, nothing himself, beholds
Nothing that is not there and the nothing that is.

Most readers meeting *The Snow Man* will immediately see it as difficult in that it does not allow them to take a 'prose' hold at first reading. There is, however, imaginative contact with the 'thingness' of the poem. There is emotional contact with the music, with what Stevens calls in *It Must Give Pleasure* 'the luminous melody of proper sound'. There is the intuition that something more than a landscape is being presented, that this is a 'poem of the act of the mind'. Whether consciously or not, the reader picks up the signal of the title. *Snow Man* instead of 'snowman' prompts an adjustment of response, the first step of the revision enacted and demanded throughout the poem.

The poem consists of a single expanding sentence. The reader gets lost partly because of his natural tendency to take the end of a stanza as a resting-point, with the result that he fails to keep pace with the sentence. In order to keep pace he has to see the sentence whole, to learn to 'perform' the sentence as well as to follow the words. It is rather like trying to sight-read a new piece of music. Until the player has decoded the notation and can obey it without stumbling, the music cannot get through.

The sentence begins with two co ordinate clauses which take the poem as far as *January sun*. The two clauses have the same structure: a main clause extended by a subordinate with a double object. The reader will sight-read the syntax correctly and supply without stumbling the missing element 'must have' in the second coordinate clause. What is probably not noticed at first is that already an act of revision is being invited in three ways. Firstly, *a mind of winter* invites thinking, though what follows is apparently simple seeing. Secondly, in the three-fold identification of what is seen, the reader also is required to be more specific in his attention to the objects. The conventional *crusted* is revised in the more original *shagged* and *rough*. Thirdly, *regard* is replaced by *behold*. *Behold* revises the neutrality of *regard*, implies more serious attention, brings connotations of wonder.

What may now cause a stumble in the reader's pace is *and not to think*. He may be momentarily misled by the semi-colon and not recognize immediately that this is a coordinate of the subordinates *to regard* and *to behold*. But this is a minor stumble, and once it is corrected, the reader, because of the meticulous normality of the syntax, keeps pace easily with the rest of the sentence. The rest of the sentence is an extension of the new coordinate *and not to think*. The method of extension again employs a pattern of recurrence: in the third and fourth stanzas repetition of phrase structure as well as of words; in the fifth stanza the two coordinates *who listens* and (who) *beholds*; the three *nothings* and the 'mirror' structure of the last line. The recurrence is creating the sound-texture. It is also maintaining the act of revision started in the two opening stanzas. *The sound of the wind* is revised in *the sound of a few leaves* which is then revised in *the sound of the land*; the *some bare place* is revised by the addition of *the listener*.

The reader keeps pace with the syntax, but not so easily with the meaning. He is hindered by the fact that the ambiguity of *must* in the first line accompanies his reading up to the last two lines. Up to *listens in the snow* two meanings appear to be open to him. One might be paraphrased: a man would need to have a mind as cold as the snow itself not to be reminded of the fact of unhappiness when he looks at a winter landscape. This is plausible because the reader is accustomed to finding pathetic fallacy in verse. The other: the essential thing is to reach a state of detachment which prevents one from seeing the physical world in terms of the human world. The two final lines remove the choice of meaning. The pathetic fallacy interpretation has to be discarded. The state *one must have* is the opposite state of *not* seeing what is not there, of *not* hearing —unlike Wordsworth—'the still sad music of humanity'.

Discarding one interpretation clears the way for exploring the implications of the second. Again, the revisionary syntax of the *and not to think* extension is the key. Firstly, there is the revision of the persona of the poem. The indefinite *one* becomes the specified *listener*. This more precise identification is foregrounded by the indicative *listens* and *beholds*. Secondly, *listens* replaces *regard* and brings with it connotations of purposeful attention. *Behold* is repeated and thus foregrounded. Thirdly, there is a new syntactic element introduced in *nothing himself*. This may be expanded into (being) *nothing himself* or (since he is) *nothing himself*. Either way the structure is not paralleled elsewhere in the poem, which has the effect of foregrounding it. It is further foregrounded in the double repetition of *nothing* in the final line.

These three revisions disclose the complexity of the key metaphor—*a mind of winter*. One might put it that the act of the poem is to 'unmetaphor' that opening metaphor and thus to enact the desired purging of mental sight. The change from *one* to *listener* foregrounds the distinction between human observer and the landscape he is part of. The pairing of *listens* and *beholds* asserts the necessity of both thinking and feeling, will and intuition, in the act of attention. (I am reminded of Lawrence's: Thought is 'man in his wholeness wholly attending'.) The foregrounding of *nothing himself* confronts the reader with the paradox that because the listener is nothing, he can see clearly what is really there and know that it is nothing.

Does the difficult adventure of this poetic sentence come then only to a nothingness, a negation of value in the human enterprise? A Macbeth vision of life 'signifying nothing'? The reader who has worked so hard is not satisfied to leave it at that. He seeks another revision, tries to hold the whole in focus, not just the final lines. Certain things emerge as he too *listens* and *beholds*. *A mind of winter* is not easily achieved: it takes *a long time*. There is a willed thrusting forward from neutral regarding to whole attentiveness. Within the final lines the affirmative *listens* and *beholds* work against the negatives. The whole poem declares the active presence of the beholder/listener. The ultimate state of being nothing is also the state of ultimate perception, a state of power as well as helplessness. The power of language itself is enacted in an exactly structured sentence. The man who is *nothing himself* is also the man who is capable of conferring identity and substance on nothing, of making it *the* nothing.

The reader's endeavour enables him to participate in an act of rigorous feeling and thinking. He does not simply make contact with meaning, but experiences a mind in the act of coming to meaning. Stevens persuades the reader to make an effort of attention which causes him also to see a little more clearly. The continual revision required by the poem brings him to perceive the continual revision living humanly demands.

One of the great pleasures of Stevens's poetry for the experienced reader is the presence of other poets. Some touch of the pleasure is possible in this poem for senior students. A Wordsworth link has been mentioned already. They will surely know Keats's *To Autumn* and thus be able to pick up the echo of the reduction of sense-experience to hearing. If they know Tennyson's *Morte d'Arthur*, there is the echo of 'a wind that shrills all night in a waste land where no one comes'. If they have studied *Richard II*, they will remember the 'mockery king of snow'—a rich echo for a reader familiar with the play.

A reader and a poet

A valuable project at senior level is independent study of the work of some poet, past or present. The choice of poet is left to the individual student. The only proviso is that the poet should not be one whose work is already being studied in class. If a very prolific poet is chosen, a selected edition is used.

Students keep a journal of the progress of dialogue with their chosen poet. The bulk of the work takes the form of the draft record. General instructions would run like this:

First simply read through the poems, letting the voice make itself heard. (Try reading some poems aloud.) Record your impressions; note the poems that particularly strike you in this sampling. Then read more slowly. Notice what changes occur in the way certain poems strike you now. Try to identify how the poet sees the world, what he values, what moves, saddens, angers him. What is distinctive about his attitude to craft, about the way he uses language? How might he answer the question: What is a poet's job? Put the work aside for a few weeks. When you take it up again, turn to your favourite poems. Has anything changed in the interval? Unwrite a short poem. How do you see your poet in relation to other poets, past or present? Choose an aspect of the work to write up in essay form. (For this section there would be some reading of criticism, suggested by the teacher.) Think back to what first prompted you to choose your poet. What has dialogue with his mind meant for you?

References

Chapter One
1 Hampshire, Stuart. Review of *The Case for the Arts*, Harold Baldry, *Times Literary Supplement* 26 February 1982.
2 Vygotsky, L.S. *The Psychology of Art*, Camb. Mass. M.I.T. London 1971.
3 Bateson, F.W. *English Studies Today* ii, Berne 1961.
4 Walsh, William. *The Use of Imagination*, Chatto and Windus, 1959.
5 Peterkiewicz, Jerzy. *The Other Side of Silence*, OUP, 1970.
6 Eliot, T.S. 'Dante', *Selected Essays*, Faber, 1951.
7 Wilson, R.A. *The Miraculous Birth of Language*, Guild Books, Dent, 1941.
8 Nowottny, Winifred. *The Language Poets Use*, The Athlone Press, University of London, 1962: indispensable study of language at work in poetry.
9 MacNeice, Louis. *Snow*.
10 See Sutton, William. A. ed. *Newdick's Season of Frost*, State University of New York Press, 1976.
11 Lerner, Laurence ed. *Reconstructing Literature*, Blackwell, 1983.
12 Darbyshire, A.E. *A Grammar of Style*, Andre Deutsch, 1971.
13 Keats, John. *The Letters of John Keats*, 2 vols. ed. Hyder E. Rollins, Cambridge University Press, 1958.
14 Gardner, Helen. *The Business of Criticism*, OUP, 1957.

Chapter Two
15 See Hourd, Marjorie. 'The Repression Stage of Adolescence', *The Education of the Poetic Spirit*, Heinemann, 1949.
16 Cary, Joyce. *Spring Song and Other Stories*, Michael Joseph, 1960.

Chapter Three
17 Edwards, Alison. 'Poetry and the Child in the Secondary School', *Presenting Poetry*, ed. Blackburn, T., Methuen, 1966.
18 Wimsatt, W.K. *Hateful Contraries*, University of Kentucky Press, 1965: helpful chapter, 'What to Say about a Poem'.
19 Hopkins, G.M. *The Letters of Gerard Manley Hopkins to Robert Bridges*, ed. Abbott, C.C., Oxford University Press, 1955.
20 Pound, Ezra. *Literary Essays*, ed. Eliot, T.S., Faber, 1954.
21 Eliot, T.S. *Four Quartets*, Faber, 1945.
22 Moore, Marianne. 'Poetry', *Collected Poems*, Faber, 1951.
23 Auden, W.H. 'A Shilling Life', *Collected Shorter Poems*, Faber, 1950.
24 *English Poets*, Chaucer, *The Prologue*, Argo PLP 1001.
25 Graves, Robert. 'The Cool Web', *Collected Poems*, Faber, 1965.

26 Spouge, William. 'Teaching Oral and Written English in Non-selective Secondary Schools', *A Common Purpose*, ed. Squire, J.R., National Council of Teachers of English, Illinois, 1965.

Chapter Four
27 Sapir, Edward. Quoted in (47).
28 Cluysenaar, Anne. *Introduction to Literary Stylistics*, Batsford, 1976: clear readable introduction to the subject.
29 Quoted in *The Man and the Mask*, Ellman, R. MacMillan, 1949.

Chapter Five
30 *Lines Written in Kensington Gardens* (Matthew Arnold), *The Fallow Deer at the Lonely House* (Thomas Hardy).
31 Ability rating of the writers: the first high, the second average, the third below average.

Chapter Six
32 Culler, Jonathan. 'Literary Competence', *Essays in Modern Stylistics*, ed. Freeman, Donald C., Methuen, 1981.
33 Daiches, David. *Critical Approaches to Literature*, Longman, 1956: valuable reference book for teachers and senior students.
34 Fowlie, W. 'In Tribute to Saint-John Perse', *Poetry*, Jan. 1961.
35 Butler, Christopher and Fowler, Alastair. *Topics in Criticism*, Longman, 1971: Excellent source book for seminar topics.
36 Sansom, Clive. *The World of Poetry*, Pheonix House, 1959.
37 Winters, Yvor. *Collected Poems*, Carcanet Press, 1978.
38 Stevens, Wallace. See *Modern Poets on Modern Poetry*. ed. Scully, James, Collins, 1966.
39 Akhmatova, Anna. Foreword to 'Requiem', *Requiem and Poem without a Hero*, trans. D.M. Thomas, Paul Elek, 1976.
40 Miles, Josephine. *The Continuity of Poetic Language*, University of California Press, 1951.
41 Empson, William. *Some Versions of Pastoral*, Chatto and Windus, 1968: substantial extract in (33).
42 Bowra, C.M. *The Romantic Imagination*, OUP, 1950.
43 Eliot, T.S. *Selected Prose*, ed. Hayward, John, Penguin, 1953.
44 Southam, B.C. *A Student's Guide to the Selected Poems of T.S.Eliot*, Faber, 1968.
45 Philippe, Charles-Louis. Quoted in (44).
46 Eliot, T.S. *The Waste Land: A Fascimile and Transcript of the Original Drafts* ed. Eliot, Valerie, Faber, 1971.
47 Leech, Geoffrey N. *A Linguistic Guide to English Poetry*, Longman, 1969: excellent account of the linguistic approach.
48 Winters, Yvor. *Forms of Discovery*, Swallow, 1967.
49 See Witemeyer, H. *The Poetry of Ezra Pound* University of California Press, 1969.

Appendix

A selection of poems for the strategies suggested in Chapter Two.

1—Noises on and off. 2—Connections. 3—A shape for feeling.
4—Tales of every day and every night. 5—Documents plus. 6—'The picture of nobody'. 7—Listening in to the world.

Sources are given for poems not listed in the Index of Poems, *qv*.
Additional symbol: MPMV—*Many People, Many Voices*, ed. Hidden, N. and Hollins, A., Hutchinson, 1978.

P. Appleton *The Responsibility*, **1**, **3**, **7**.
W.H. Auden *O what is that sound?* Tst2, **1**, **4**.
J. Berry *A Visit to Jamaica* MPMV. **4**, **5**, **7**.
E. Bishop *The Fish* V2, Tst 3, RB, **2**, **6***; Songs for a Colored Singer* RB. **6**.
W. Blake *The Chimney Sweeper* **4**, **5**; *Infant Sorrow* RB. **3**, **7**.
E. Braithwaite *Limbo* MPMV. 1; *Slow Guitar* MPMV. **1**, **3**.
A. Brownjohn *In this city* TTW. **3**, **4**, **6**.
N. Cameron *The Compassionate Fool* RB. **3**.
C. Causley *Cowboy Song* V2, **1**; *Timothy Winters* V2, Tst 3, TTW. **5**.
C.P. Cavafy *As Much as You Can* RB. **7**.
N. Chakrabarti *The Old Man of Birmingham* MPMV. **5**, **7**.
J. Clare *July* Tst3, **2**, **5**; *The Lout* Coll. **2**, **5**, **6**.
e.e. cummings *Buffalo Bill's* RB. **1**.
J. de Graft *An Un-African Breakfast* MPMV. **1**, **5**.
W. de la Mare *Napoleon* RB, **7**.
E. Dickinson *A narrow fellow in the grass* **2**, **4**; *I never hear the word 'escape'* Coll. **3**, **6**.
K. Douglas *Vergissmeinicht* **4**, **5**, **7**.
D. Dunn *On Roofs of Terry Street* **2**, **4**, **5**.
R. Frost *Beyond Words* V2. **3**, **6**; *Fire and Ice* Tst5. **1**, **3**.
R. Fuller *Little Fable* **4**, **6**.
R. Graves *Brother* V2. 4; *Traveller's Curse* V2. 3; *Welsh Incident* **4**.
T. Gunn *Baby Song* RB. **1**, **6**; *On the Move* EM. **5**, **7**.
D. ap Gwillyn *The Rattle Bag* RB. **1**, **3**.
T. Hardy *The Fallow Deer at the Lonely House* RB. **4**, **6**; *Heredity* Tst5, V2, RB. **6**.
S. Heaney *The Forge* Tst4. **1**, **2**, **5**; *Death of a Naturalist* **3**, **6**.
M. Holub *The Lesson* Tst4. **7**.
T. Hughes *Public Bar TV* V3. **2**, **5**; *November* **2**, **5**, **6**.
R. Jarrell *The Death of the Ball Turret Gunner* RB **1**, **6**.
J. Kirkup *The Blind Boy* RR **2**, **6**.

D.H. Lawrence *Two Performing Elephants* Drag, RB, VI, **2**, **5**;
   Wages EM. **5**, **6**.
L. Lerner *The Experiment* MPMV. **7**.
D. Levertov *Merritt Parkway* V3. **1**, **5**; *What were they like?* V3. **7**.
F.G. Lorca *The Six Strings* RB **1**, **2**, **3**.
G. MacBeth *Bats* VI, Drag. **2**.
H. MacDiarmid *Another Epitaph* RB. **7**.
R. McGough *My Bus Conductor* V3, **5**, **6**.
L. MacNeice *Bagpipe Music* RB, 1; *Christmas Shopping* EM, **5**.
T.Y. Malik *Offal* MPMV. **4**, **5**.
A. Mikhailov *If you've never been . . .* RR. **7**.
A. Mitchell *Autobahnmotorwayautoroute* RB. **1**, **5**; *Watch your step—I'm
   drenched* RB. **5**.
O.M. Mtshali *Keep off the Grass* MPMV. **2**, **5**.
E. Muir *The Horses* RB, RR, Tst5, **7**.
O. Nash *Old Men* RB. **6**.
W. Owen *Strange Meeting* **7**.
B. Patten *You'd better believe him* Drag. **3**, **4**, **6**; *The Projectionist's Nightmare*
   Drag, Tst4, PW. **2**, **5**.
J. Pilinszky *Fable* RB. **3**, **4**.
J. Prévert *Exercise Book* EM. **1**, **3**, **5**.
P. Redgrove *Spring* Tst3. **2**.
E.A. Robinson *Reuben Bright* **4**, **5**.
C. Sandberg *Snatch of Sliphorn Jazz* V3. **1**; *Phizzog* V2, **1**, **6**; *Fog* VI,
   Drag, EM, **2**.
S. Smith *Bog Face* RB. **1**, **3**, **6**; *Not waving, but drowning* Tst5. **3**, **6**.
W. Soyinka *Telephone Conversation* **4**, **5**.
W. Stafford *Judgements* V3, **5**, **6**, **7**; *Ice-Fishing* V3. **1**, **2**, **5**.
D. Thomas *The Hand that Signed the Paper* RB. **2**, **7**.
E. Thomas *The Gallows* **1**, **3**; *Out in the Dark* RB. **2**, **6**.
A. Waley *Plucking the Rushes* RR, Tst5, V3, **3**, **5**; *A Protest* Tst5, V2. **7**.
S. Weöres *Monkeyland* RB. **1**, **3**, **7**.
H. Williams *The Builders* Drag. **2**, **5**.
Y. Yevtushenko *The Companion* **4**, **5**, **7**; *Schoolmaster* EM, **6**, **7**.

Further Reading

Tunnicliffe, S. *Poetry Experience*, Methuen, 1984: excellent suggestions
for classroom activity; contains valuable section 'Sources and
Resources'.
For the section 'Listening in to the world', see also the following:
Bosley, K. *et al. Russia's Other Poets*, Longman, 1968.
Index on Censorship (Magazine) Writers and Artists Educational Trust,
   39c Highbury Place, London N5 1QP.

Index of poems and sources

Numbers refer to pages in this book. Selected sources are given for most poems. For other sources see that invaluable reference book: *Where's That Poem?* compiled by Helen Morris Blackwell (rev. 1985).

Drag — *Dragonsteeth*, Eric Williams, Edward Arnold, 1972.
EM — *Every Man Will Shout*, R. Mansfield & I. Armstrong, OUP, 1964.
PW — *Poetry Workshop*, M. & P. Benton, Hodder & Stoughton, 1975.
RB — *The Rattle Bag*, S. Heaney & T Hughes, Faber, 1982.
RR — *Rhyme and Reason*, R. O'Malley & D. Thompson, Chatto & Windus, 1957.
Tst — *Touchstones*, 5 vols., M. & P. Benton, Hodder & Stoughton, 1971.
TTW — *Tunes on a Tin Whistle*, Alan Crang, Wheaton, 1967.
V — *Voices*, 3 vols., Geoffrey Summerfield, Penguin, 1968.
Coll — *Collected Poems*.

E. Dickinson   *A bird came down the walk* Tst3, V1, **33**; *A narrow fellow* PW, RB, RR, Tst4, **39, 54**; *A root of evanescence* Coll, **52**; *Because I could not stop for Death* Tst5, **65–7, 85–6**; *I'm nobody* V1, **19**; *I started early* Tst2, **16**.

J. Donne   *Death, be not proud* RR, 57, **93–4**; *The Good-Morrow* **86–8**.

K. Douglas   *Landscape with Figures* Tst5, **62**; *Vergissmeinicht* TTW, **78**.

K. Dunn   *On Roofs of Terry Street* Drag, PW, **33**.

T. S. Eliot   *Macavity* RB, **58**; *Selected Poems*, **103–109**.

R. Frost   *Desert Places* RB, V3, **19**; *Home Burial* V3, **36**; 'Out, out,—' PW, RB, TTW, V2, **33–4**; *Stopping by Woods* RB, **51–2**; *The Runaway* Drag, PW, Tst3, **78**.

R. Fuller   *Little Fable* Drag, **33**; *The Image*, **37**.

M. Gilmore   *Nationality* V3, **21**.

O. Goldsmith   *Elegy on the Death of a Mad Dog*, **58**.

R. Graves   *A Civil Servant* Tst4, V2, **35**; *The Beach* Tst3, **11–12**; *Welsh Incident* EM, RR, V2, **54**.

T. Hardy   *At the Railway Station* V1, **78**; *During Wind and Rain* Tst5, **83**; *Neutral Tones* Tst5, **86–8**; *The Clock-Winder* V3, 13; *The Darkling Thrush* RB, RR, **55, 56**; *The Going* Coll, **57**; *The Voice* Coll. 57.

S. Heaney   *Blackberry Picking* Drag, PW, V2, **50**; *Dawn Shoot* Tst4, **37**; *Death of a Naturalist* PW, Tst5, V2, **41–2**; *The Diviner* Tst3, **34**.

A. Hecht   *More Light! More Light!* RB, TTW, 21, **64–5**.

G. Herbert   *Love* Tst4, **89**; *The Collar* Tst5, **60–1**.

R. Herrick   *To Daffodils*, **59–60**.

J. Hewitt   *Turf-carrier on Aranmore* V1, **16**.

P. Hobsbaum   *The Place's Fault* PW, RR, Tst4, **36**.

M. Holub   *A Boy's Head* V3, **19**; *A History Lesson* RB, Tst4, **21**; *Bullfight* RB, **78**; *How to Paint a Perfect Christmas* V3, **78**.

G. M. Hopkins   *Felix Randall* TTW, V3, **93–4**; *Pied Beauty* RB, RR, Tst4, **39**; *Spring* RB, Tst4, **47, 93–4**.

T. Hughes   *Hawk Roosting* EM, **38–9**; *Pike* Drag, **39–40**; *November* Tst4, **39**.

F. Juhász   *Birth of a Foal* RB, **78, 79**.

P. Kavanagh   *In Memory of my Mother* Coll, **93–4**.

J. Keats   *Chapman's Homer*, 30–31; *To Autumn*, **42–5**.

P. Larkin   *Take One Home* RR, **78**; *The North Ship* RB, **59, 79**; *The Whitsun Weddings* TTW, **90**.

D. H. Lawrence   *Humming-Bird* RB, **52**; *Snake* RB, 27; *What Is He?* V3, **19, 34**.

J. Logan   *The Picnic* Tst5, TTW, V3, **86–8**.

E. Lucie-Smith   *The Lesson* Tst3, **49**.

G. MacBeth   *The Bird* Tst3, **28–9**; *The Wasps' Nest* Drag, Tst4, **37**.

N. MacCaig   *Aunt Julia* RB, **34**; *Frogs* V3, Tst4, **79**.

H. MacDiarmid   *Perfect* PW, RB, **41, 98**.

L. MacNeice   *Autobiography* RB, **53**; *Prayer before Birth*, **61–2, 93**.

A. Marvell   *To His Coy Mistress* Tst5, **90**.

J. Milton   *On His Blindness*, **55–6**; *Paradise Lost* Book One **100–102**.

E. Muir   *Sick Caliban* Coll, **21**; *The Combat* Coll, **16**.

T. Nashe   *In Time of Pestilence* RB, RR, **55**.

W. Owen   *Anthem for the Doomed Youth* V3, **61**; *Futility* RB, Tst5, V3, **89**; *Strange Meeting* RB, V3, **62–3**; *The Sentry* Tst3, V3, **54–55**.

S. Plath   *Mushrooms* PW, RB, Tst3, V2, **28**; *Pheasant* RB **37–8**.

A. Pope   *The Rape of the Lock*, **98–9**.

E. Pound   *Fan-piece, for her Imperial Lord*, **108–9.**

P. Redgrove   *Thirteen Ways of Looking at a Blackboard* Tst4, **11**.

H. Reed   *Naming of Parts* RR, Tst5, TTW, **62**.

E. A. Robinson   *Reuben Bright* V2, **41–2**.

C. Rowbotham   *Dissection* PW, **50**.

W. Shakespeare   *Shall I compare thee*, **61, 86–8**; *Winter*, **12**.

P. B. Shelley   *Ozymandias* RB, RR, **89**.

J. Skelton   *Woefully Arrayed* Tst4, **55**.

C. Smart   *My Cat, Jeoffrey* RB, Tst3, V1, **27**.

W. Soyinka   *Telephone Conversation* V3, **36**.

W. Stafford   *Travelling through the Dark* TTW, V2, **89**.

J. Stallworthy   *First Blood* Drag, Tst4, V2, **37**.

W. Stephens   *Earthy Anecdote* RB, **94**; *The Show Man*, **112–15**.

J. Suckling   *Why so pale . . .* RR, **86–8**.

M. Swenson   *Was Worm* V1, **39**.

J. Swift   *A Gentle Echo* RR, **52-3**.

A. Tennyson   *The Eagle*, **51**.

D. Thomas   *And death shall have no dominion* RB, **93**.

E. Thomas   *The Gallows* Drag, V1, **37, 53**; *The Owl* RB, RR, **91**.

R. S. Thomas   *A Peasant* TTW, **93–4**.

A. Thwaite   *Sunday Afternoons* Drag, **36**.

C. Vallejo   *Masses* RB, **21**.

F. Villon   *Ballade* V3, **21**.

R. Warner   *Nile Fishermen* EM, TTW, **50–1**.

R. Wilbur   *A Fire Truck* V2, **62**.

W. C. Williams   *Landscape with the Fall of Icarus*, **93–4**; *The Red Wheelbarrow* V1, **11**.

W. Wordsworth   *A slumber did my spirit seal*, **110–13**; Extract from *The Prelude* RB, **89**.

W. B. Yeats   *The Fisherman* Coll, **70–72**; *The Wild Swans at Coole* EM, **83–4**.

Y. Yevtushenko   *The Companion* TTW, **88–9**.